LIFE LIBRARY OF PHOTOGRAPHY

Light and Film

BY THE EDITORS OF TIME-LIFE BOOKS

TIME-LIFE BOOKS, NEW YORK

ON THE COVER: Three elements make up basic tools of the photographic process: light, represented by a 300-watt bulb; a sensitive material, here a segment of 35mm film; and one of the photographer's means of controlling the interaction of the two, a 10-zone gray scale used to translate the tones of the natural world into a manageable range of gray shades in a photograph.

Contents

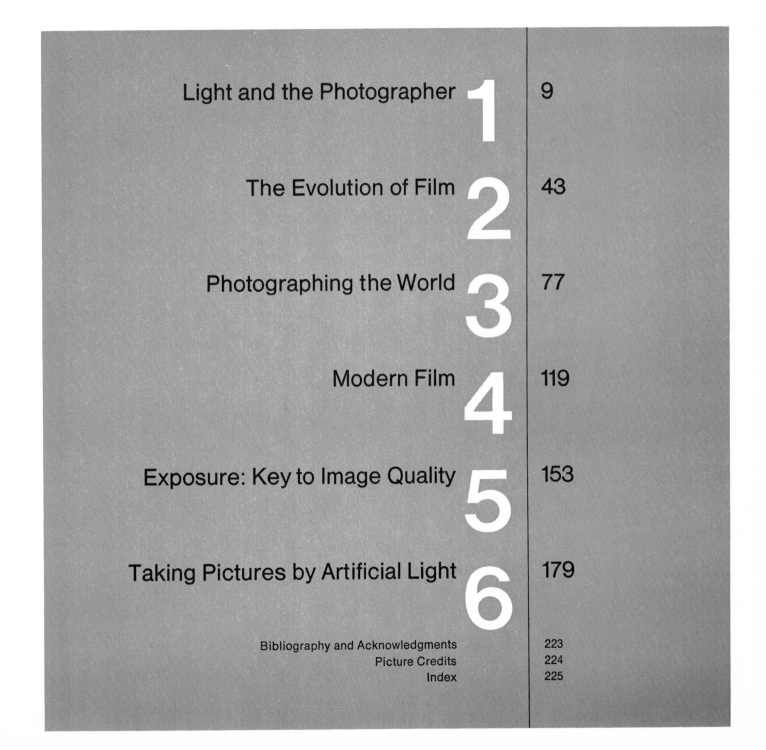

TIME-LIFE BOOKS

FOUNDER: Henry R. Luce, 1898-1967

Editor-in-Chief: Hedley Donovan
Chairman of the Board: Andrew Heiskell
President: James R. Shepley
Group Vice President: Rhett Austell

Vice Chairman: Roy E. Larsen

MANAGING EDITOR: Jerry Korn
Assistant Managing Editors: Ezra Bowen,
David Maness, Martin Mann, A. B. C. Whipple
Planning Director: Oliver E. Allen
Art Director: Sheldon Cotler
Chief of Research: Beatrice T. Dobie
Director of Photography: Melvin L. Scott
Senior Text Editor: Diana Hirsh
Assistant Art Director: Arnold C. Holeywell
Assistant Chief of Research: Myra Mangan

PUBLISHER: Joan D. Manley
General Manager: John D. McSweeney
Business Manager: Nicholas J. C. Ingleton
Sales Director: Carl G. Jaeger
Promotion Director: Paul R. Stewart
Public Relations Director: Nicholas Benton

LIFE LIBRARY OF PHOTOGRAPHY

SERIES EDITOR: Richard L. Williams
Editorial Staff for *Light and Film:*
Editor: Robert G. Mason
Assistant to the Editor: Simone Daro Gossner
Text Editors: James A. Maxwell,
Peter Chaitin
Picture Editor: Carole Kismaric
Designer: Raymond Ripper
Staff Writers: George Constable,
Peter Wood
Chief Researcher: Peggy Bushong
Researchers: Maureen Benziger,
Rosemary Conefrey, Monica O. Horne,
Sigrid MacRae, Shirley Miller,
Don Nelson, Kathryn Ritchell
Art Assistant: Jean Held

Editorial Production
Production Editor: Douglas B. Graham
Assistant Production Editors:
Gennaro C. Esposito, Feliciano Madrid
Quality Director: Robert L. Young
Assistant Quality Director: James J. Cox
Copy Staff: Rosalind Stubenberg (chief),
Ruth Kelton, Florence Keith, Pearl Sverdlin
Picture Department: Dolores A. Littles,
Barbara S. Simon, Lora T. Moore
Traffic: Carmen McLellan

Valuable aid was provided by these individuals and departments of Time Inc.: TIME-LIFE Photo Lab, George Karas, Herbert Orth; Editorial Production, Norman Airey; Library, Benjamin Lightman; Picture Collection, Doris O'Neil; Photo Equipment Supervisor, Albert Schneider; TIME-LIFE News Service, Murray J. Gart; Correspondents Elisabeth Kraemer and Renee Houle (Bonn), Maria Vincenza Aloisi (Paris), Margot Hapgood (London), Ann Natanson (Rome), Traudl Lessing (Vienna), Mary Johnson (Stockholm), Robert Kroon and Alex des Fontaines (Geneva), Martha Haymaker (Los Angeles).

Once a photographer has a camera in his hands he comes up against a formidable array of technical and esthetic choices. Which film to use? How should he light the scene—with natural illumination, flash or floodlights? How should lighting angles be fixed relative to the camera for pleasing results? What f-stop and shutter speed will capture the minute detail and subtly shaded tones that a fine photograph needs?

Even an experienced photographer is often hard put to answer these questions confidently. The reason they seem so complex is that all are interrelated.

A decision on illumination always affects exposure, and the choice of film may change the other decisions. The questions also seem (or sometimes have been made to seem) mysterious because they all involve that remarkable physical quantity, light, and its reactions with the more substantial materials of the world—and most particularly with certain compounds of silver on the surface of photographic film.

The mystery disappears and the complexities begin to fall in place when the basic facts about light are understood. This volume in the LIFE Library of Photography deals with the nature of light; the evolution of modern film since the early discoveries of light's effect on sensitive substances; the types of film now available and their uses; light meters and their operation in the determination of accurate exposure; sources of artificial light; and the creation of pleasing light patterns. These topics cover the basic problems faced in taking a photograph. By exploring them in orderly fashion this book shows how the technical objectives of a "good" negative can be combined with the esthetic aims of an outstanding picture.

The Editors

Light and the Photographer 1

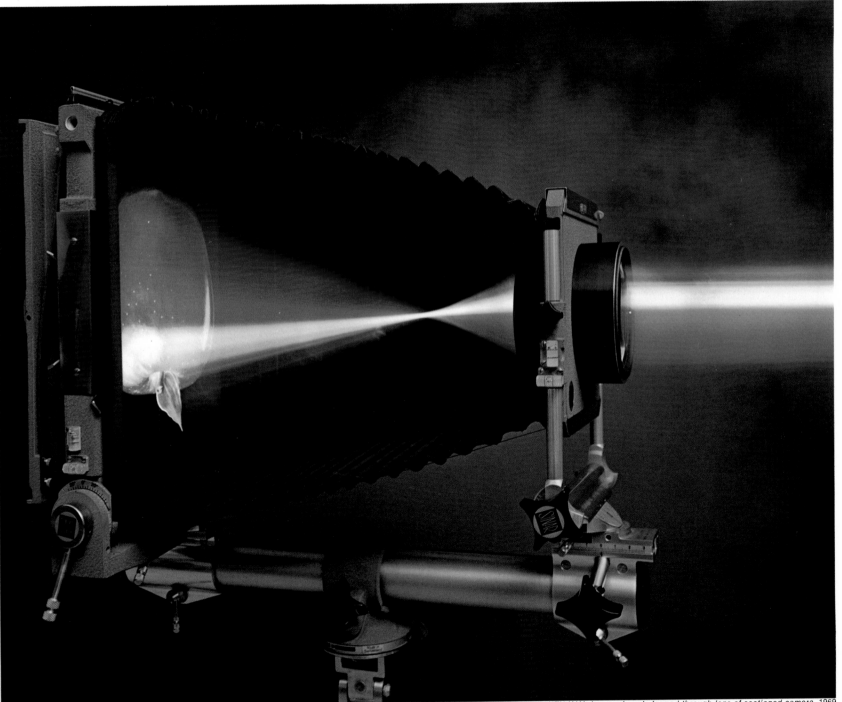

KEN KAY: *Image of apple formed through lens of sectioned camera,* 1969

How Light Acts

Anybody who is old enough to take pictures understands that photography depends on light. Obviously, the film is exposed by the light that enables the eyes to see. But the dependence of photography on light goes far deeper than that and takes forms that are not nearly so obvious, for the character and quality of a picture can be altered by the character and quality of the light. The source of the light matters—the sun makes different pictures from those incandescent bulbs do (and fluorescent lights give results that are yet again different). The color of the light—and all light is colored even though the human eye seldom notices—affects not only color pictures but black-and-white ones too. Material substances—clothing, walls, a lake surface —react with light and alter its reaction with photographic film. Even the very air we breathe, invisible though it is, may have marked effects on photographs—effects that vary with the time of day.

Many of these influences of light on photographs are at first surprising. What you see with your eyes is not what you get with the camera. The explanation lies in the nature of photographic film. It does not work like the light-sensitive retina of the eye, and more important, it lacks the brain that interprets retinal signals to complete the act of "seeing." These discrepancies can ruin a picture for the unwary photographer—or create startling effects for the photographer who deliberately takes advantage of them. The most common example is the color transparency shot indoors with "outdoor" type film; it comes out with an all-over red tinge. The reason: light from ordinary incandescent bulbs is redder than daylight and the color film records it as it is while human sight does not (the brain automatically counterbalances the reddish color of the illumination).

When black-and-white film is used, the influences of the quality of light are subtler. All ordinary black-and-white films are sensitive to some light the eye cannot see and they are also more sensitive to blue-colored light and less sensitive to red-colored light than the eye is. In a photograph of a landscape, for example, a deep blue sky can turn out a blank white and a pale red flower may have blossoms almost as dark as its leaves. These departures from what seems natural to the eye can be compensated for—or deliberately emphasized—if the photographer understands a few basic facts about light and its reactions with the material substances of the world.

Light is usually described as a form of energy, and it is indeed a kind of electromagnetic energy little different from radio waves, television signals, heat and X-rays. All are made up of waves that spread, bend, interfere with one another and react with obstacles much in the manner of waves in water. But if you ask a physicist what light is, he may answer that it, together with all its electromagnetic relatives, is really a form of matter, little different from substantial things such as houses. Like them, it is made up of individual par-

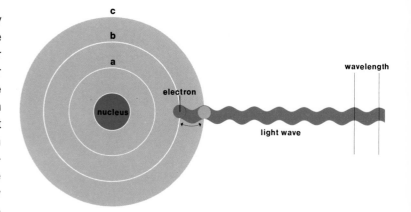

Light originates inside an atom such as the hydrogen atom diagrammed above, when one of the atom's components, an electron, oscillates in a way that is symbolized as a back and forth movement between two positions. This oscillation begins with the absorption of energy from outside the atom. Some absorbed energy goes to increase the energy content of the electron, a jump in energy that is represented as a shift of the electron from its location within the atom (orbit b) to another location (orbit c). But the higher energy levels—the orbits farther from the atom's nucleus—are less stable. The electron, like a ball lifted to a precarious spot on a narrow shelf, quickly drops back to a lower level (orbit b). The energy that is lost in this change appears as a light wave, and the wavelength of the light (marked off by parallel lines on the drawing of the waves) is established by the difference in energy between the two orbits. In the case of the hydrogen atom, the electron movement indicated produces light with a wavelength the eye senses as red.

ticles. The light particles, called photons, travel in streams in much the same way as droplets of water pouring from a hose; when a photon hits something it delivers a noticeable jolt, just as water droplets do.

There seems to be a paradox here. Can light be both energy and matter, wave and particle? The answer is yes and the reasons are not complicated. All energy is a form of matter; Einstein's famous equation $E=mc^2$ (E referring to energy and m to the mass of matter) is one indication of this fact. What is more, all matter has some characteristics of waves and some characteristics of particles. The wave characteristics of ordinary matter such as houses are rarely discernible and can generally be ignored; ordinary matter usually acts as if it were made up of particles. When it comes to the kind of matter we call light, however, the situation is quite different. Light's wave characteristics are predominant in many instances—and in yet other instances the particle characteristics reveal themselves. When light reacts with photographic film, for example, it acts like a particle: a photon strikes a molecule of silver bromide or silver iodide and partially disrupts it to make the exposure *(pages 124-125).* But in the majority of the phenomena involved in photography, light can be described as acting like a wave, and most discussions of light in this book will refer to light waves rather than to photons.

There are three major characteristics of a light wave that concern photographers: (1) its intensity, which is related to the height of the wave crests and indirectly determines brightness of the light; (2) the wavelength, which depends on the distance between crests and largely determines color; and (3) its polarization, the angular orientation of the crests, which can be exploited for special photographic purposes. All three characteristics are influenced by what happens when light waves interact with ordinary substances: air, metal and glass surfaces, clouds, photographic filters. It is this light-matter reaction, beginning with the actual generation of a light wave inside an atom in the sun or a light bulb *(opposite),* that creates all the effects we see—and the sometimes quite different effects we photograph.

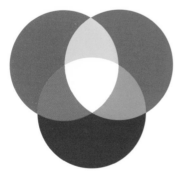

Any color can be simulated by mixing light waves of red, green and blue of varying intensities. Each hue is determined by its dominating wavelength and mixed wavelengths combine visually. Thus red plus green combine to produce yellow. All three make white.

The Electromagnetic Spectrum

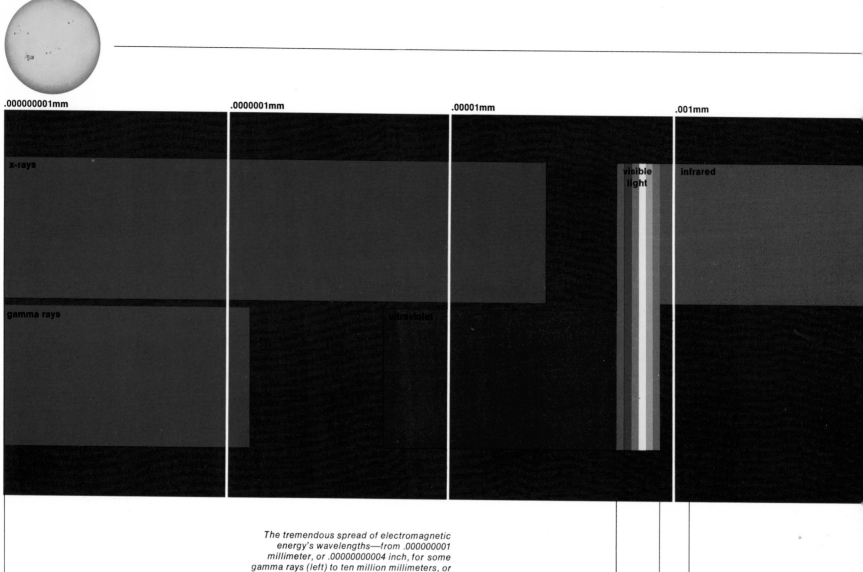

.000000001mm .0000001mm .00001mm .001mm

x-rays

gamma rays

ultraviolet

visible light

infrared

The tremendous spread of electromagnetic energy's wavelengths—from .000000001 millimeter, or .00000000004 inch, for some gamma rays (left) to ten million millimeters, or about six miles, for longer radio waves in the spectrum shown—is divided rather arbitrarily into groups. The divisions overlap since they depend partly on wavelength and partly on the way the waves are generated or used; thus waves of the same length are called X-rays if emitted by an X-ray tube but gamma rays if emitted by an atomic reaction. Only waves of the small group within the brackets at right are properly called light because they alone stimulate nerve endings in the human eye (ultraviolet waves can be seen by bees). Photographic film, however, can be made sensitive to all waves from the shortest wavelengths (bracket at left) to some in the infrared group (bracket at far right).

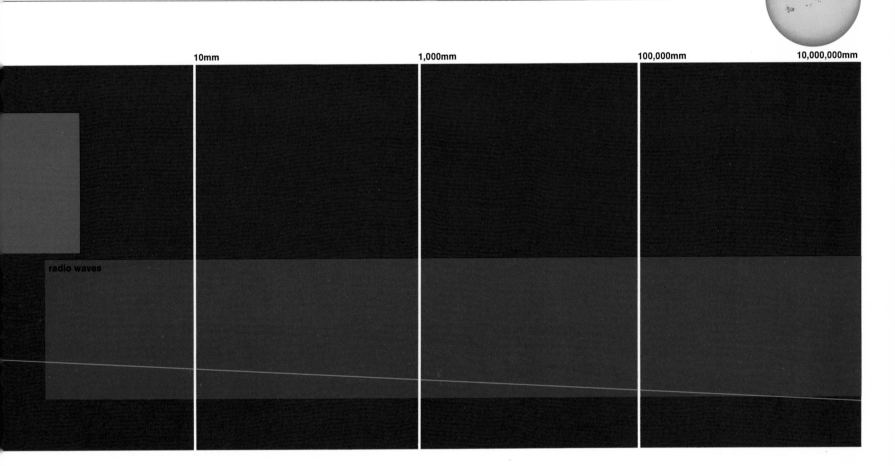

10mm   1,000mm   100,000mm   10,000,000mm

radio waves

it seems strange to think of light waves as being almost the same as radio waves, and yet the only physical difference between them is their length. Radio waves are the longest among the broad range of electromagnetic energy waves listed above, with wavelengths as great as six miles. At the other extreme of the electromagnetic spectrum, gamma rays, produced by disintegrating atoms of radioactive elements, have wavelengths of less than approximately .000000004 inch. The visible light waves are a very small group near the middle of the spectrum with wavelengths ranging from .000016 to .000028 inch.

Within the narrow range of visible light, each individual wavelength is emitted by the sun, but greenish wavelengths are emitted in greater intensity than are the others. This mixture registers in the brain as white. But other sources of light balance their wavelengths in different ways. Electronic flash tubes and fluorescent lamps emit light that may be made up of a relatively small number of distinct wavelengths —a mixture of a few distinct colors; unless these wavelengths combine to simulate sunlight (as they do in many flash units), they produce unnatural results in color photographs. Incandescent bulbs emit a range of wavelengths, as the sun does, but the range is an unbalanced one, containing more of the long wavelengths (red colors) than it

does of the short ones (blue colors).

The wavelength balance is dependent on temperature; the sun's temperature cannot be matched by incandescent filaments, and they cannot produce as many short wavelengths as the sun. The resulting reddish cast in their light must be counterbalanced for color pictures and allowed for in black-and-white photographs.

But even sunlight is not always what it seems. It includes wavelengths that are not visible light, yet do affect film. And any of its wavelengths, visible or invisible, may be absorbed, separated, re-mixed and re-emitted on their way through the air to the earth—and to the film in the back of a camera.

15

The Earth's Atmospheric Screen

Before there was life on earth, nearly all the sun's electromagnetic waves managed to reach the surface of the earth at one time or another. With life came a new kind of atmosphere, which now screens out most of the solar wavelengths shorter than visible light (which is fortunate since short waves can damage human tissue). The way and the degree to which the other wavelengths are able to get through depends on the atmosphere's content of carbon dioxide, smoke, dust, clouds, moisture and even on the time of day —with effects on photographic film that are sometimes annoying, sometimes surprising, sometimes beautiful.

The atmosphere screens out short wavelengths because of the way they react with matter. When short wavelengths strike molecules in air they release some of their energies, which are converted to another form. In many cases, they energize the molecules' electrons, causing them to jump to higher energy levels; when these electrons fall back they release energy that eventually takes the form of heat. Short wavelengths have then been converted into a different form of energy—they have been absorbed.

This happens only to the shortest wavelengths. Those that are not absorbed in this way include (a) a few too short to be seen, (b) all those in the visible spectrum and (c) many of those too long to be seen. The shortest of the invisible rays that get through the atmosphere in any quantity are in the group called ultraviolet. These affect all ordinary films (color as well as black and white) in the same way visible light does. Among the longer wavelengths that are invisible is the group called the infrared—they have wavelengths just longer than the deepest visible red. These infrared rays are detected by special film and prove very useful in photography. Infrared film can be used to take pictures through a layer of clouds, since many infrared waves are not absorbed by cloud particles. Needing no visible light, such film—when exposed to infrared waves—can take pictures in the dark (to trap a thief) or in dim light (to photograph a church wedding). And infrared film records natural objects, which reflect infrared differently than they do visible light, in some quite unnatural but surprisingly beautiful tones *(pages 148-149).*

Not all the waves that penetrate the atmosphere slip through unaffected. They, too, give up energy to molecules in air, but not in a way that causes energy-level jumps. When the energy is released, it is often altered in some way —in the direction of travel, the angle of undulation or in wavelengths. Since wavelength affects color, it is this reshaping of transmitted waves that gives sky, clouds and sunsets their colors.

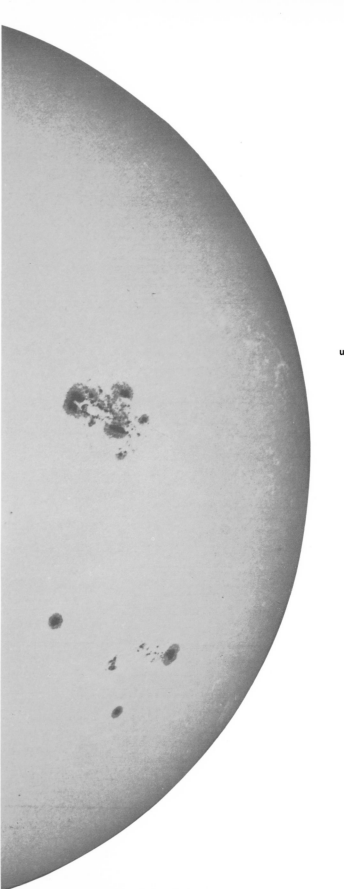

ultraviolet

blue

green

red

infrared

Only a few electromagnetic waves of short wavelength in the invisible ultraviolet group (top) penetrate the earth's screen of air. Most of the still shorter waves—the dangerous gamma and X-rays—are absorbed in the upper atmosphere. The longer visible waves, a range of wavelengths—colors—that combine to register in the brain as white, pass through most molecules in air but may be altered or partially blocked by pollutants, moisture and clouds. Many of the still longer infrared waves (bottom), which are invisible to the human eye, are little hindered by the atmosphere's contents and some of them even pass readily through clouds.

Scattering: Key to Sky Colors

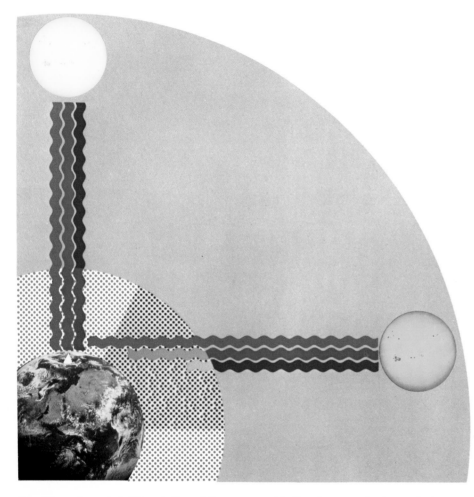

The distance the sun's light travels through the atmosphere, changing with the time of day, causes its alterations in hue. At noon the sun is directly over an observer standing at the point indicated by the arrow and its rays pierce the narrow band of atmosphere perpendicularly. The molecules in air scatter more of the short blue waves, but less of the longer green or the still longer red ones, which pass through. The sun then appears yellow (because a

combination of green and red waves looks yellow) and the sky is blue. At sunset, the light reaches the observer obliquely, traveling through much more atmosphere. It has encountered more molecules and more scattering takes place—so reducing the proportion of short (blue and green) wavelengths that the longer reddish ones predominate; the sky then takes on a red tinge and the sun looks a bright yellow-orange.

The spectacular color of the sunset at right is caused by the same phenomenon that makes the sky blue: the selective scattering of light waves by molecules of air (and very small dust and water particles). When these molecules react with light waves passing by, they affect the shorter wavelengths (bluish colors) more than the longer ones (yellow and red), bouncing them around and giving the sky its bluish tinge.

When to an observer on earth the sun appears low in the sky, near the horizon —as at sunrise and sunset—its light travels a greater distance through the atmosphere than when it is overhead *(diagram at left).* Traversing more air molecules, the light waves undergo more scattering. So many of the shorter waves are scattered that relatively few get straight through to an observer; the waves that do get through are mostly the longer yellow and red wavelengths and, therefore, the sun appears yellow-orange. Sunsets in a clear cloudless sky are generally unimpressive, but when a beam of this reddish light paints the clouds it produces spectacular displays like the one at the right.

Not only is the color of the sun when it is low in the sky different from its appearance during the rest of the day, but the quality of the overall illumination is different, too. Because more of the rays from the sun are scattered around through the atmosphere at sunrise and sunset, the balance between the brightness of sky light and of direct sun rays becomes more even than it is at midday. The sky light brightens shadows and softens the contrast between light and dark areas to create the delicate illumination photographers prize.

HARALD SUND: *Sunset, Rocky Mountain National Park, Colorado*, 1969

The Varieties of Reflection

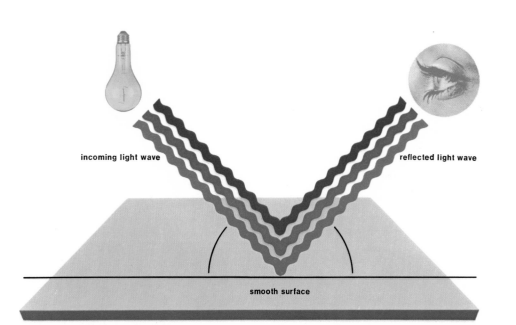

incoming light wave

reflected light wave

smooth surface

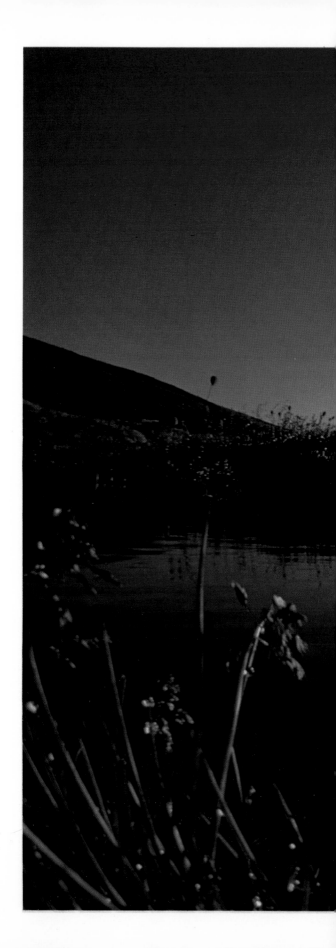

Light waves bounce off a smooth surface as a ball bounces off a wall: the angle of incidence equals the angle of reflection. All the reflected waves remain organized like the incoming ones, and the eye sees the light bulb as a reflected image. If the surface is rough, however, some waves hit and bounce at one angle, others at different angles; the reflected waves become disorganized and no image can be seen.

Light coming from the sun is unpolarized—the waves undulate at all angles, as indicated by the light and dark red waves below. They can be polarized—made to undulate at one angle, as indicated by the single pale red wave. This can happen when light waves are reflected at certain angles by such nonmetallic substances as glass and water. The part of the light that continues through the substance remains essentially unpolarized. Metals are different—their electrons have a different arrangement that does not cause reflected light waves to be polarized.

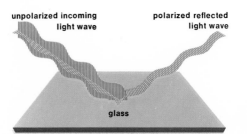

unpolarized incoming
light wave

polarized reflected
light wave

glass

Any smooth surface—polished metal or a highland pool *(right)*—bounces light waves to create a reflected image *(diagram at left above)*. Metals send the incoming waves back out essentially unchanged, which is why they make good mirrors. But certain nonmetallic substances such as diamonds, glass and water have a different electron arrangement and reflect differently in ways important to photographers. Their electrons are interrelated, each layer with the one behind, so that light energy striking the surface electrons is partially passed along to those behind; the result is a dim reflection. When a nonmetal's electrons are so closely interrelated, the waves they release can undulate at the same angle *(left)*. Even this dim reflection can be killed by a thin coating of another material—the antireflection coating used on camera lenses. The electrons in the coating reverse the reflected waves and pass them, too, to electrons in the rear.

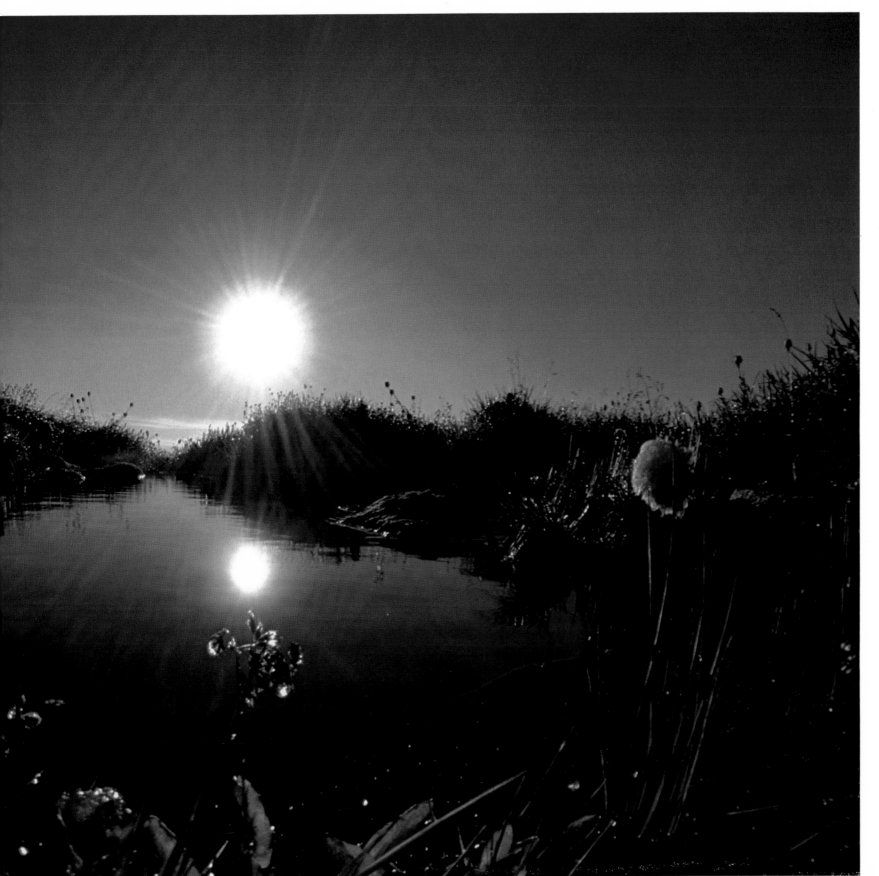

HARALD SUND: *Sunrise over Highland Pool, Mount Evans, Colorado,* 1969

Bending Waves by Refraction

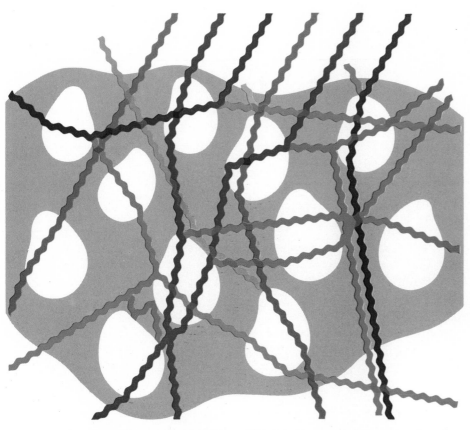

A substance composed of transparent particles —such as clouds or sugar—is diffusely luminous instead of transparent because of the way light is reflected at the particle surfaces and refracted, or bent, inside the particles. If the light reaching the particles (top) is a mixture of wavelengths—which gives white light—a similar mixture emerges (bottom) with the directions of its waves altered (hence the diffusion).

Clouds are transparent water droplets —yet they usually look the way they do at right, a diffuse white instead of transparent. Refraction, the bending of light, is one reason.

When the light waves enter or leave a droplet they bend so that they zigzag through the cloud and emerge in many directions. Reflections at the droplet surfaces also change waves' directions, adding to the disorganization and giving the cloud a diffuse white look.

Glass also bends light by refraction, but does not look white—unless it is finely powdered. When it is solid, as in a camera lens, it produces only a few controlled changes of direction and the light waves remain organized.

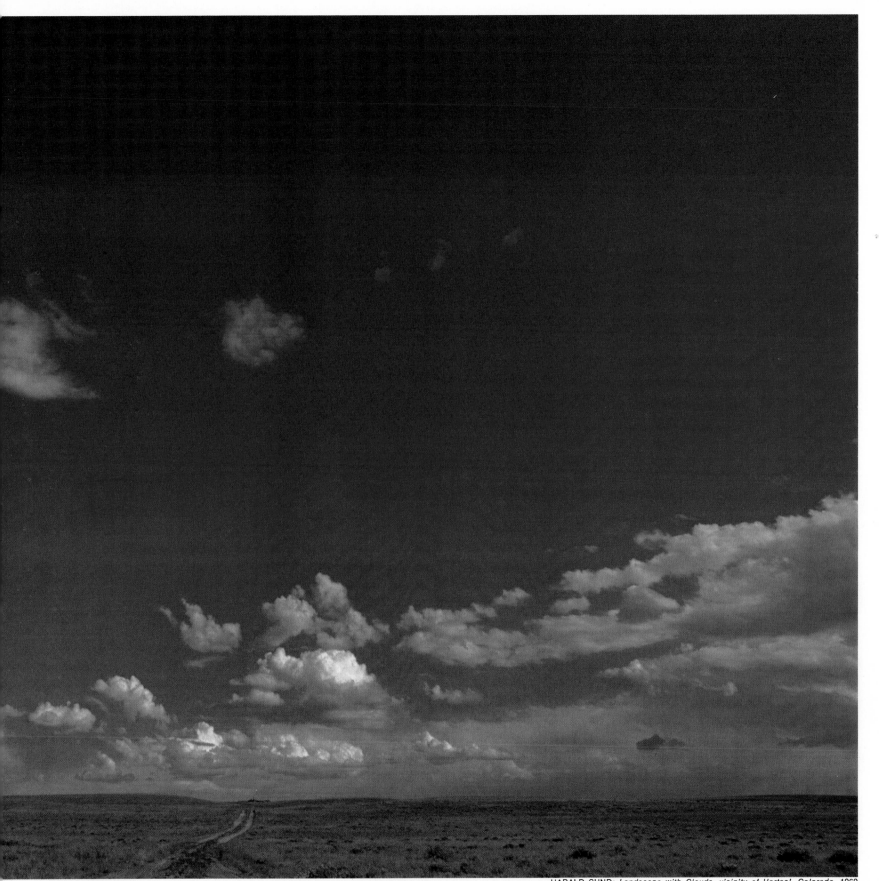

HARALD SUND: *Landscape with Clouds, vicinity of Hartsel, Colorado, 1969*

How Filters Work

When a red filter intercepts white light —represented above by waves of red, green and blue, which together make white—it screens out the green and blue. Only red remains to be transmitted. The green and blue waves are absorbed as their energies are transferred to electrons in the filter molecules. The electrons may quickly release their newly gained energies, but usually in the form of heat rather than in that of light. The warmth produced in this manner can actually be felt after such a filter has been exposed to white light for a time.

The man-sized glass discs at the right, which are components of a piece of modern sculpture, work just like the filters a photographer places over the lens of his camera to control the film's rendition of colored objects *(pages 176-177)*. The discs achieve their multicolored effect by allowing certain wavelengths of light to pass through them while absorbing others *(diagram at left)*. Daylight—the mixture of all colors forming white light—from outside the gallery window appears variously yellow, red, blue or black, depending on which filter, or combination of filters, it is seen through.

A segment of the edge of the blue disc at right looks black because it overlaps the red behind it. Between them they absorb all colors and allow no light to pass. Yet the yellow disc, a thin sliver of which shows at the left of the picture, does not affect the color of the overlapping red disc—the red disc still looks red. Their absorption provides the explanation. Yellow glass absorbs mainly blue and transmits yellow, green and red (a combination that the brain registers as yellow). Since little red is absorbed by the yellow disc, it does not alter the appearance of the red disc in front of it.

Which wavelengths a filter absorbs are determined by molecular structure. If an orbit exists that an electron can jump to when struck by light of a particular wavelength, that wavelength is usually absorbed. Energy levels can be matched to almost any wavelength by applying modern chemical methods, and filters can be compounded to absorb a few wavelengths, a broad range of wavelengths or even several separate wavelengths in the spectrum. ☐

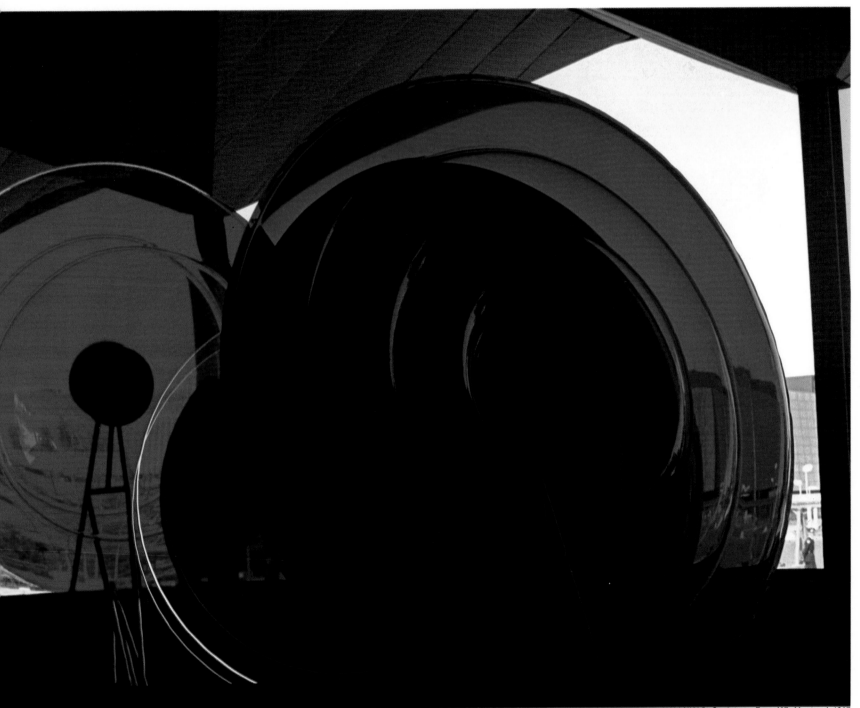

JAN LUKAS: *Sculpture, Expo '67, Montreal*, 1967

How Photographers Exploit Light

The hard, vertical line of white light that pierces the shadows in Charles Harbutt's photograph at the right demands attention. It draws the eye directly into the picture and like an arrow points to a young boy's hands pressed flat against a wall. The light and the hands convey the photographer's thought: the boy is blind; he has discovered light in the only way he can, through touch.

This picture is one of a series Harbutt made of children at The Lighthouse in New York City, an institution for the blind. Harbutt had noticed, after observing him for several days, that this painfully deprived boy used his hands to feel for the warmth created by the warm rays of the sunlight that threaded the narrow space between two buildings each afternoon at about the same time. It was the only light needed for exposure, and it made Harbutt's picture.

Like Harbutt, the photographers who took the pictures on the pages that follow used the physical characteristics of light to dramatize reality: direct sunlight for a hard, graphic image, hazily diffused daylight for a mysterious, romantic quality, directional light to accent a figure or emphasize form. They employed its qualities deliberately; no photograph shown is a lucky shot. Each results from a conscious awareness of what light can do in a photograph.

It is common for a serious photographer to spend a great deal of time at this, experimenting with light just as he does with cameras and film. George Krause is one who, like several other outstanding professionals, spent the early part of his career making all his pictures on overcast days, when the illumination was diffuse. When he felt he had mastered the use of such lighting he turned to scenes with harsher contrasts of shadow and brightness—with the stunning results shown on page 38. Such concentration on one particular aspect of light helps a photographer learn to "see" light—i.e., to visualize the differences that changes in illumination will make. With this educated and heightened sense of perception he can make a picture live up to the original Greek meaning of the word photography: "light writing." Shadows, reflections, patterns of light, even the light source itself may become the heart of a composition in which solid objects are incidental and light is the theme.

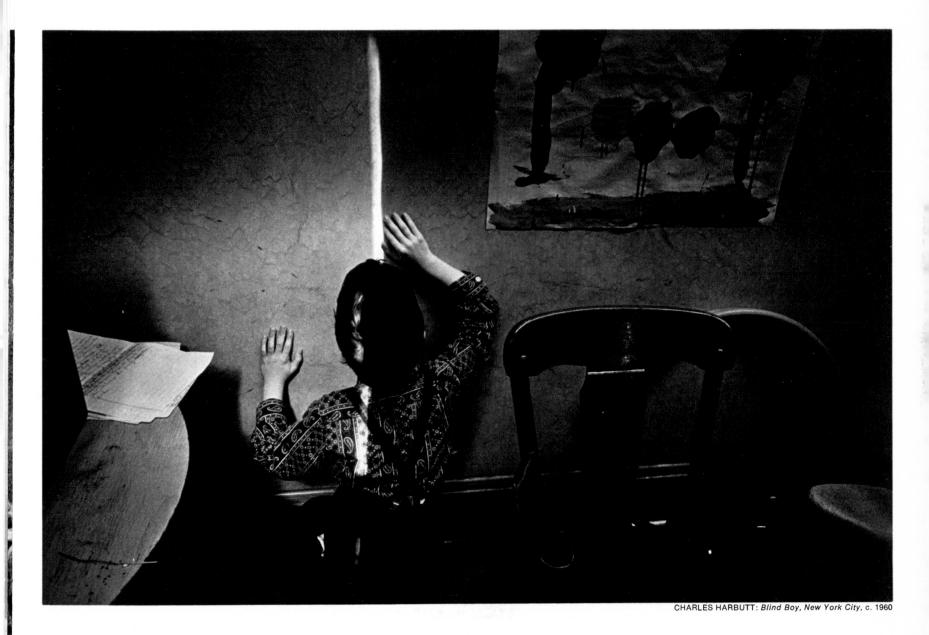

CHARLES HARBUTT: *Blind Boy, New York City*, c. 1960

Creating Mystery

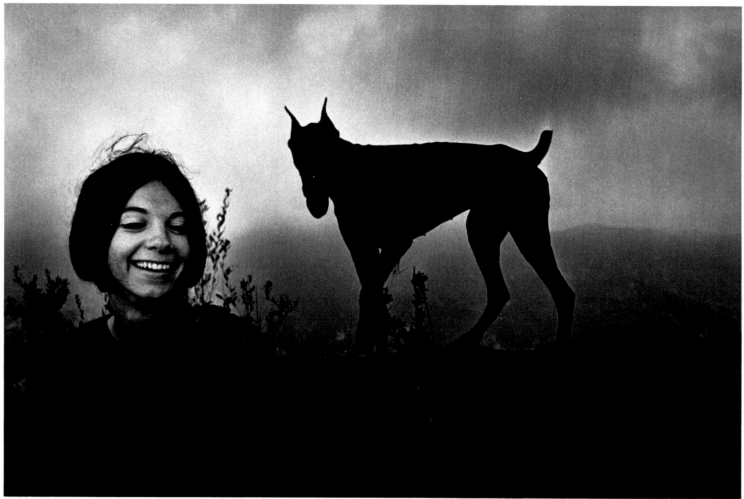

RONALD MESAROS: *Vesta, Topanga Canyon, California,* 1966

The fog was rolling in from the Pacific Ocean on the afternoon that Ronald Mesaros took a friend, his 35mm Minolta and his Doberman pinscher, Vesta, for a walk in the hills above Los Angeles. The light, filtering through the fog, was dull and nondirectional. It was barely strong enough to produce detail in the face of the girl who had accompanied Mesaros, but not sufficient to do more than outline the shape of his black dog. Taking advantage of this unusual contrast, Mesaros produced the disquieting photograph above—a smiling girl, seemingly oblivious of the sinister, featureless silhouette looming up behind her. The mood of the picture, one of tension, mystery and imminent danger, would surely dissolve in the glare of bright sunlight. ☐

The Evolution of Film 2

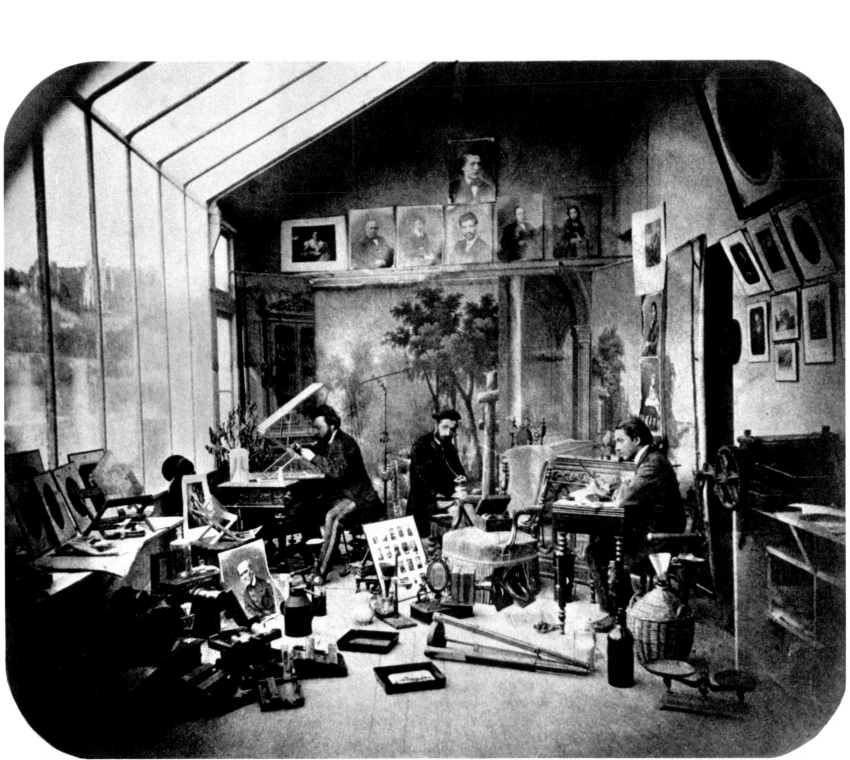

PHOTOGRAPHER UNKNOWN: *Studio of the Photographer Bourgeois, Paris,* c. 1870

phy's time had come and in England a gentleman scientist had already invented the modern photographic process. On January 25, 1839, less than three weeks after Daguerre's announcement to the French Academy, William Henry Fox Talbot appeared before the Royal Institution of Great Britain to present his negative-positive system. Talbot was a disappointed man when he gave his hastily prepared report. Daguerre's prior announcement, Talbot admitted later, "frustrated the hope with which I had pursued, during nearly five years, this long and complicated series of experiments—the hope, namely, of being the first to announce to the world the existence of the New Art—which has since been named Photography." Although Talbot could not be the first, he was determined to establish, as soon as possible, that his process was wholly independent of Daguerre's.

Talbot was fairly typical of a number of amateur scientists who graced the gentry of the early 19th Century. Born in southern England in 1800 to an upper-class family—his mother was the daughter of an earl, his father an officer in the Dragoons—Talbot received a proper education at Harrow and Trinity College, was elected a Fellow of the Royal Society for his contributions to mathematics and served briefly as a member of Parliament. He sometimes used a camera obscura to help him in sketching, one of his hobbies, and he recalled that in 1833 "the idea occurred to me—how charming it would be if it were possible to cause these natural images to imprint themselves durably and remain fixed on paper." He soon began his experiments.

Talbot's first attempts were silhouettes, produced by placing objects on light-sensitive paper and exposing them to the sun—the technique used earlier by Wedgwood. Talbot sensitized a fine grade of writing paper by dipping it into a weak mixture of salt and water, waiting for it to dry and then brushing the sheet with a silver nitrate solution. This operation was repeated several times with each sheet. But unlike Wedgwood, Talbot soon learned how to retard, if not halt completely, the fading of the image. In his experiments, he observed that sensitivity was nearly eliminated in areas of the paper where the salt concentration was excessive. He applied this discovery by dipping the exposed sheet in a concentrated salt solution. (Soon he was led to the permanent fixative that Daguerre had independently discovered, sodium thiosulfate, by his friend and fellow scientist, Sir John Herschel.)

Now Talbot carried the making of a silhouette a step further: he made a positive paper print of it. The negative silhouette—i.e., a white image of, say, a leaf, outlined by the surrounding dark areas—was placed face down on a second piece of sensitized paper. Then the two were pressed together under a pane of glass and exposed to sunlight, a procedure now known as contact printing. Light could pass through the leaf's white image on the negative and thereby create a dark image on the second sheet; meanwhile the dark areas of the negative blocked light so that the corresponding sections of the second sheet remained white. The result was a positive resembling the natural original, a dark leaf against a white background. This was the foundation for the negative-positive system of modern photography. The most important test came when Talbot applied the technique to an image recorded in a camera. After exposing a negative to an outdoor scene, he made a positive print: a recognizable picture of the scene.

With the light-sensitive coating used in these early experiments, the image could be seen forming during the exposure. Talbot simply looked at the paper under the pane of glass if he were making a silhouette, or peered through a hole in the camera if he were taking a picture, and when the negative image was sufficiently pronounced, halted the exposure. But in June 1840, about a year and a half after his appearance before the Royal Institution, Talbot announced a revolutionary advance: a new, highly sensitive negative material that recorded a latent image on paper. Nothing could be seen on this new coating after exposure, he said, but he "found that the picture existed there, although invisible; and by a chemical process . . . it was made to appear in all its perfection." Talbot called the process "calotype" from the Greek words *kalos* for "beautiful" and *typos* for "impression." (It was Talbot's friend, Sir John Herschel, who later coined the name by which the process is now known, from the Greek words *photos* for "light" and *graphos* for "drawing." Sir John was also the first to employ the words "negative" and "positive" to describe Talbot's system.)

Talbot made a number of improvements in the calotype over the next several years. By increasing the sensitivity of the coating, he was able to reduce the required exposure time, enabling him to photograph people. But there was one flaw in the paper negative, and Talbot never eliminated it completely. The fibers in the paper blocked some light during the printing operation and thus produced a soft, slightly fuzzy photograph. When the inventor began waxing his negatives to increase translucency, this distortion was almost eradicated, but the calotype's sharpness never quite matched that of the daguerreotype.

The problems of the paper negative became academic in October 1847 when Abel Niepce de Saint-Victor, an army officer and cousin of Nicéphore Niepce, appeared before the Academy of Sciences in Paris to announce his new process, one that used glass plates coated with an emulsion of a silver compound suspended in egg white. The advantages of glass over paper as a base had been apparent for some time to other experimenters; glass presented no texture problems, was uniformly transparent and chemically inert. But until Niepce de Saint-Victor used egg white, no one had found an emulsion that would hold a light-sensitive material on glass, although many

1 | The Art of Making a Daguerreotype

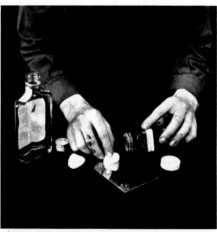

1 | cleaning the plate

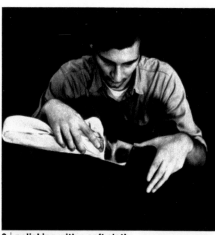

2 | polishing with a soft cloth

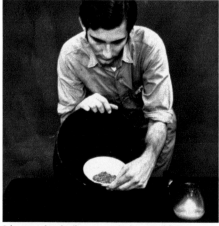

3 | preparing iodine crystals for sensitizing

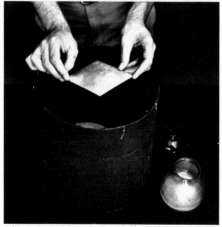

4 | sensitizing the plate

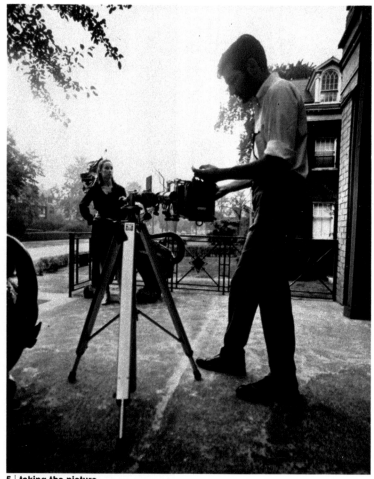

5 | taking the picture

NOTE: Because of the hazardous materials involved, readers are warned not to attempt the daguerreotype process shown here, or the wet-plate process (pages 72-73). Even the calotype process (pages 66-67) requires care to avoid silver-nitrate burns.

When Joel Snyder begins to make a daguerreotype, he remembers the advice of the inventor of the process: for good results, the plate of silver-coated copper must be spotlessly clean and highly polished. He soaks a wad of cotton in a mixture of pumice and alcohol and thoroughly cleans the surface (1). Next, he buffs the plate to a high gloss (2), using soft lamb's wool.

Now Snyder prepares to sensitize the plate by placing a bowl of iodine crystals (3) at the bottom of an airtight cylinder. With only a candle for illumination—the light level must be low during this stage—Snyder suspends the plate, silver side down, on the two wires inside the top of the cylinder (4). He leaves the plate in place for about 10 minutes, while fumes from the iodine crystals rise to the silver coating on the plate and combine with it to form the light-sensitive compound, silver iodide. To increase sensitivity, Snyder exposes the plate to fumes from a bromine-lime mixture for two minutes, then returns to the iodine for two more minutes. Finally he puts the plate into the camera and poses the model (5), his wife.

After the exposure has been made, Snyder returns to the candlelit darkroom to prepare for developing. This

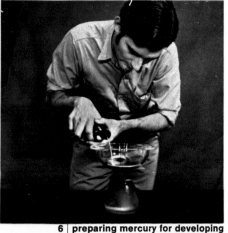

6 | preparing mercury for developing

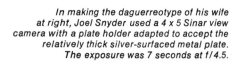

In making the daguerreotype of his wife at right, Joel Snyder used a 4 x 5 Sinar view camera with a plate holder adapted to accept the relatively thick silver-surfaced metal plate. The exposure was 7 seconds at f/4.5.

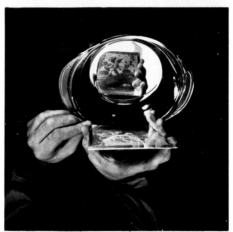

7 | the developed image

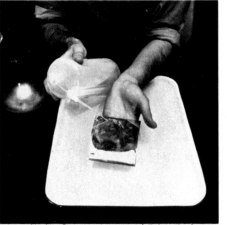

8 | fixing the image

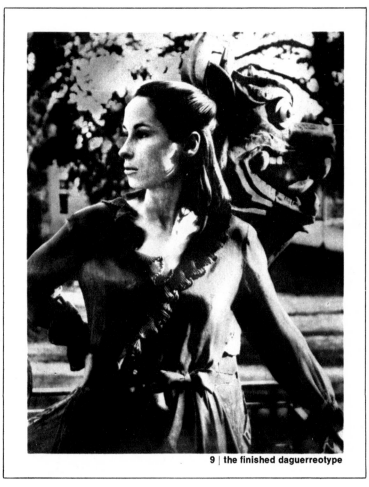

9 | the finished daguerreotype

process is carried out inside an airtight box to avoid harm from mercury fumes, but in the picture above, the box has been removed to show the steps. Snyder first pours mercury into a bowl supported above a spirit lamp (6). After putting a thermometer in the mercury and lighting the lamp, he quickly lowers it into the box and fastens the top.

He looks through a window in the box and when the thermometer shows that the mercury has reached a temperature of between 140°F. and 180°F., he places the exposed plate in a holder, unseals a slot near the top of the box and inserts the holder so that the silver side of the plate is exposed to the rising mercury fumes. The forming image can be watched by looking through the window of the box—the picture is reflected in the bowl of mercury (7). Finally Snyder pours photographic fixer (sodium thiosulfate) on the plate (8) to make the image permanent. Then he washes the plate in distilled water. The result is a sharply defined daguerreotype (9).

The Tintype: A Picture While You Wait

In 1856 soon after the introduction of the economical ambrotype, Hannibal L. Smith, professor of chemistry at Kenyon College, patented the still cheaper, quick-service tintype, which delivered a finished picture even faster than the ambrotype. The fast delivery came from new, rapid processing solutions, the low cost from the tintype's materials. Like the ambrotype, the tintype was a collodion wet-plate negative on a dark background, which resulted in a positive image. But instead of a glass plate backed with dark cloth or varnish, Hannibal used a metal sheet, usually thin iron enameled black or chocolate brown, to support the collodion.

The inexpensive tintypes quickly became the rage of the era. Enterprising tintypists appeared everywhere, taking pictures of children in parks, of families at company picnics, of newly married couples outside churches. Hundreds of thousands of young men, self-conscious in their new uniforms, posed stiffly for the tintype camera before going off to the Civil War. The results were generally crude, but in the hands of a talented photographer the tintype process could produce striking portraits such as the one at right.

Although no copies could be made of tintypes, many photographers used special multi-lensed cameras to take several pictures at once and accommodate anyone who wanted extra photographs of himself. Even after roll film and the simple box camera made every man his own photographer, tintype purveyors prospered. They were fairly common in the United States as late as the 1930s and a number of practitioners are still to be found in South America and other parts of the world. ☐

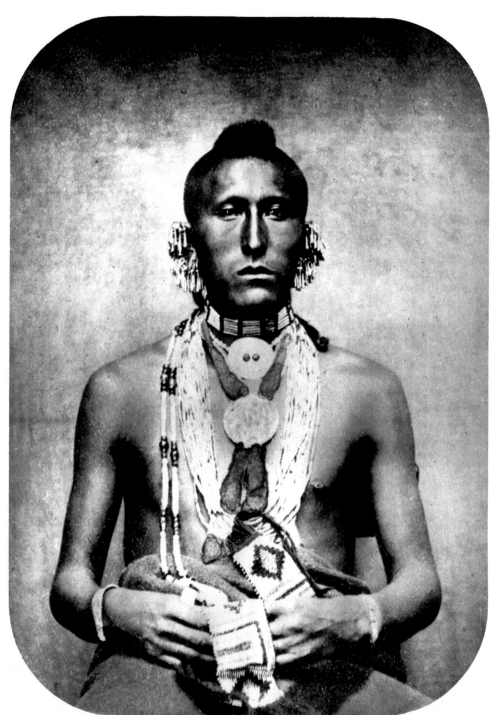

PHOTOGRAPHER UNKNOWN: *Portrait of an Indian,* c. 1860

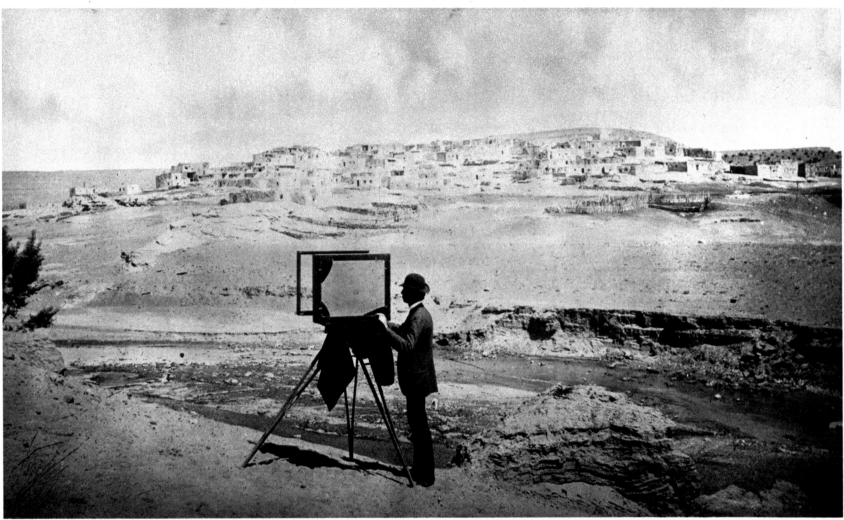

PHOTOGRAPHER UNKNOWN: *William Henry Jackson, with his 20 x 24-inch view camera, photographing Zuñi Pueblo near Laguna, New Mexico,* c. 1877

Recording an Era

In May 1842 a gigantic fire swept through Hamburg, Germany, killing 100 persons, destroying more than 4,000 buildings and rendering a fifth of the population homeless. Almost before the embers were cold, two photographers, Carl F. Stelzner and Hermann Biow, were picking their way through the rubble of the gutted city. Loaded down with a heavy camera, silvered plates, dark tent, chemicals and sensitizing and development equipment, they made 40 daguerreotypes of the aftermath of the tragedy *(opposite page)*. Their pictures, taken only three years after the birth of photography, were probably the first news photographs in history.

Stelzner and Biow were among a rapidly growing body of photographers who saw their role as basically that of reporters, conveyors of information about the world and times in which they lived. To them, immediacy and reality were the major strengths of photography, not its ability to render "art" in paintinglike landscapes, still lifes or contrived allegorical tableaux. During the first half century or so after Daguerre had startled the world with his invention, these pioneers blazed the trail of what we now call documentary photography. Their subjects were as varied as the world itself: heads of state juggling the destiny of nations and housewives haggling with street vendors; bloody conflicts and placid scenes in village squares; the ruins of ancient civilizations and the growth of new ones; faraway places and familiar cities. Burdened with their cumbersome paraphernalia, these photographers climbed mountains and descended into mines, went aloft in balloons, crossed deserts, navigated unexplored rivers and risked their lives on battlefields to bring back pictures people wanted to see.

Although there were no means of reproducing these pictures directly in newspapers and magazines until the half-tone mechanical process for making engravings from photographs was developed late in the 19th Century, they enjoyed a surprisingly wide audience. Many people bought prints singly for their private collections. Others acquired books—*Egypt, Sinai and Palestine; Mont Blanc and its Glaciers*—with the photographs painstakingly pasted to the pages. Eventually weekly news journals began copying photographs and printing the results in the form of wood engravings. But the greatest popularity of documentary photographs came in mid-century with the invention of the stereoscopic camera, which made a pair of views that were printed together, side by side, on one card. Looked at through a special viewer, or stereoscope—one of the most popular was designed by the Boston humorist, physician and photography buff, Oliver Wendell Holmes—the two pictures merged to create a scene with three-dimensional depth. The oak-trimmed stereoscope and its stack of 3-D picture cards became a standard adjunct to the Victorian parlor, providing millions of people with a new and exciting concept of their world.

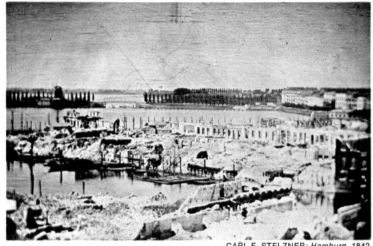

CARL F. STELZNER: *Hamburg*, 1842

Making the world's first news photographs, Carl F. Stelzner took this daguerreotype of the 1842 Hamburg fire from a rooftop near the Elbe River to show the ruins in the Alster district. In the foreground the banks of a canal are strewn with the rubble of buildings, docks and a bridge.

Although portraits and travel photographs were what most people wanted to buy, men like Stelzner and Biow quickly recognized the unique ability of the camera to freeze a moment in time, to record an important happening with such authenticity that anyone looking at the photograph felt almost as though he were witnessing the event. For the first time, through photography, a clerk in London, a mechanic in Boston or a waiter in Paris could be present, at least vicariously, at such historic occasions as the coronation of King Wilhelm of Prussia, the great gathering assembled on St. Peter's Square to hear Pope Pius IX proclaim the doctrine of papal infallibility or the signing of a peace treaty in China by mandarins and British representatives.

Such early news photography probably had its greatest public impact in the reporting of war. When the United States and Mexico fought in the late 1840s, photographers were on hand to take pictures of the troops on both sides. At about the same time, a photographer recorded a Russian army of occupation that had come to help the Austro-Hungarian Empire control rebellious Hungarians. But these ventures produced only a few stilted pictures of soldiers in formation. Modern reportage of war was born and matured in the decade between 1855 and 1865, the years when photographers went to the battlefields of the Crimean War and the United States Civil War. The ways in which the two conflicts were documented differ enormously, as can be seen in the work of the photographer most closely connected with each war: Roger Fenton, who was with the British, French and Turkish forces in the Crimea, and Mathew Brady, who headed the photographic teams that accompanied the Union armies fighting the Confederacy.

Fenton's war was fought in the hills and valleys of the Crimean borderland between Russia and Turkey. Russian expansionist pressures had led Turkey to declare war in October 1853; the following March England and France became allies of the Turks. Shortly before England entered the conflict, a British publication, *The Practical Mechanics' Journal,* proposed that photography be used "to obtain undeniably accurate representations of the realities of war and its contingent scenery, its struggles, its failures and its triumphs." Combat artists had illustrated battle scenes before, but the work of the painter, the *Journal* said, "is powerless in attempting to describe what occurs in such operations, whilst a photographic picture brings the thing itself before us." In its enthusiasm for the essential "truth" of photography, the *Journal* overlooked the fact that the photographer chooses which "truths" will be his subjects.

England had been at war for about a year when Roger Fenton, a 35-year-old lawyer and amateur artist-photographer, was personally selected by Queen Victoria and Prince Albert to go to the Crimea (the venture was financed by the Manchester publishing house of Thomas Agnew & Sons).

The royal couple had little, if any, interest in Fenton's photographing "the realities of war" and certainly none in his recording "its failures." On the contrary, he may have received explicit instructions to avoid that sort of thing; the home-front populace was already getting too much of it from newspaper reporters on the scene.

During the autumn of 1854 and the winter that followed, the British press was filled with stories about the dreadful conditions under which the troops lived and the almost criminal maladministration of the war. William Howard Russell of *The Times* of London was especially vehement. In late November he wrote that the men were in the midst of a winter campaign without warm, waterproof clothing and that "not a soul seems to care for their comfort, or even for their lives." In a December dispatch he wrote: "The dead, laid out as they died, are lying side by side with the living. . . . The commonest accessories of a hospital are wanting . . . for all I can observe, these men die without the least effort being made to save them." Casualty lists bore out such grisly accounts. Of the men who died in the Crimea, seven eighths were victims of cholera and exposure; only one eighth died in battle. Just before Fenton was to leave for the war in early February 1855, popular outrage forced the resignation of the incumbent prime minister, Lord Aberdeen. In this highly volatile political situation, the Queen almost surely ordered Fenton to take no pictures that would further arouse the anger of the citizens.

Fenton and his two assistants arrived at Balaclava in the Crimea on March 8, 1855. With them they brought a van that had been converted into a combination darkroom and living quarters, and 36 large cases containing five cameras, a number of lenses of different focal lengths, some 700 unsensitized glass plates, chemicals, a still for purifying water, printing frames, a stove, food, wine, harnesses for four horses and a set of carpenter's tools. Fenton would be using the relatively new wet plates, which had to be prepared immediately before use but permitted considerably shorter exposures than earlier materials.

In Balaclava, Fenton was shocked by the indifference to even elementary sanitation. "The whole place is one great pigsty," he wrote. "At present eighty sheep are slaughtered every day in the vessels in harbour alone, and the entrails thrown into the water alongside. All over the camp, animals wanted for food are killed close to the tents, and the parts not used are rotting for days." However, such scenes, which would have offended Victorian tastes as well as Victoria herself, were not subjects for Fenton's camera.

In contrast to the soldiers, Fenton lived fairly well during the months he was in the Crimea. He was welcomed into the top military circles, where good food, vintage wines and other amenities were routine. But in his work he shared the danger and hardship of the front. His van, painted a light color

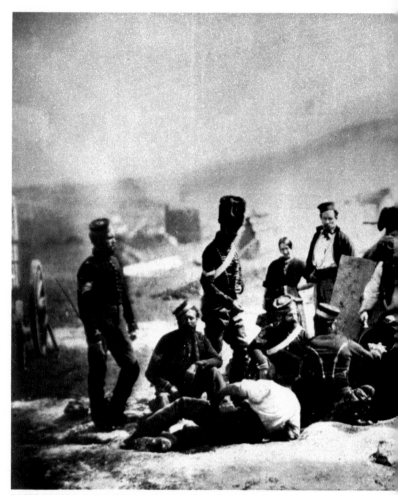

ROGER FENTON: *Field Kitchen of the 8th Hussars, the Crimea,* 1855

The war in the Crimea appeared comfortable enough in Roger Fenton's pictures of nattily uniformed soldiers being served a meal in the field and the neat encampment of an artillery unit (opposite). What they failed to record was the other face of the conflict: men in inadequate clothing shivering in the cold and rain, abominable sanitary conditions that led to cholera epidemics—and the theatrical military bumbling, pain and wholesale death that marked this "last of the gentlemen's wars."

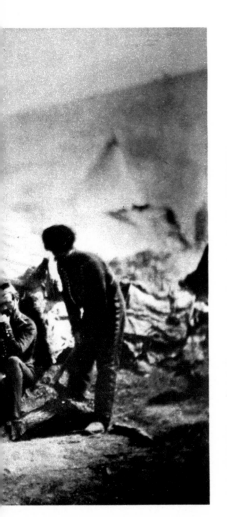

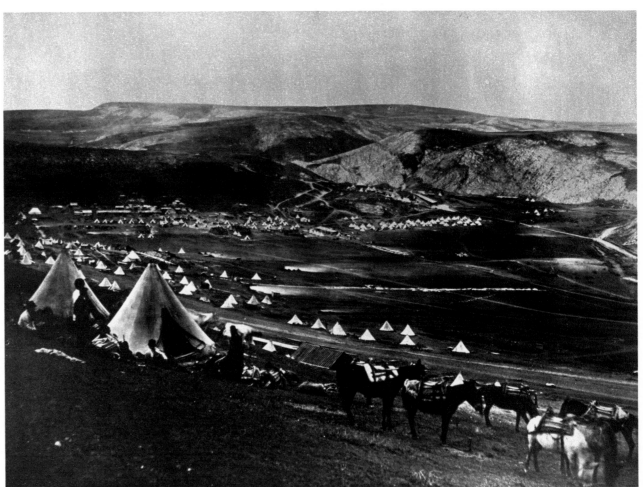

ROGER FENTON: *Encampment of Horse Artillery, the Crimea, 1855*

to reflect heat, could be seen for miles on the battlefield; it frequently became the target of Russian artillerymen, who probably thought it was an ammunition wagon. On one occasion, a shell tore off its roof. Fortunately Fenton and his assistants were not injured. A far worse trial for the photographer and his helpers was the intense, dry heat of early summer and the accompanying dust and swarms of flies. The van became an oven that cooked the men and their materials. "When my van door is closed before the plate is prepared," Fenton wrote, "perspiration is running down my face, and dropping like tears. . . . The developing water is so hot I can hardly bear my hands in it." All the darkroom work became extremely difficult. Cleaning plates became a major problem. Minute foreign substances on the glass, which created no difficulties in more moderate temperatures, now reacted chemically to the heat and caused spots and streaks on the negative. Coating large plates with their emulsion was a maddening task. Even though the collodion was thinned, it often dried where it was first poured before the edges were covered. And when a plate was properly prepared, the collodion would frequently dry—drastically reducing its sensitivity—within the few minutes required to insert the plate in a frame, get it to the camera, take the picture and return to the darkroom for development.

Despite such handicaps, Fenton took many excellent pictures *(pages 82-83)*. He was unable to capture action because of the relatively long exposure required even by wet plates, but his photographs of officers and men look remarkably spontaneous and unposed. They reveal, however, a highly selective view of war—a war without death or destruction, without horror or suffering or fear. We see an officer about to enjoy a glass of wine after a hard day in the field, a group of soldiers teaching a dog to sit up, gunners taking a siesta near a mortar. Only a few pictures, such as "The Tombs of Cathcarts Hill" (a half dozen or so headstones and men raising a flag) and "The Valley of the Shadow of Death" (a deserted road strewn with cannonballs) offer even a slight reminder that war is a lethal business.

Although men who had served in the Crimea may have had reservations about Fenton's one-sided portrayal of the war, Queen Victoria, her government and the British public apparently had none. When Fenton returned to England in July 1855, he was warmly received by the royal family and arrangements were immediately made to exhibit his several hundred pictures in London and other English cities. Portfolios of prints were published and single pictures were also put on the market. In terms of counteracting, at least partially, the effects of the grim reporting and casualty lists from the Crimea, Fenton's mission was a success.

In the early summer of 1861, just six years after Fenton had returned to London, President Abraham Lincoln, deeply immersed in plans for the first major battles of the Civil War, took time to listen to the request of a photographer and then to scribble a two-word note: "Pass Brady." By granting the famous portrait photographer, Mathew Brady, permission to travel anywhere with the Union armies, Lincoln cleared the way for a kind of photographic recording of war never seen before *(pages 96-103)*.

Pictures of wars and other news events brought the realities of life home to millions for the first time. But once over, such realities were soon forgotten; Brady, for one, could hardly sell a war picture after the conflict came to an end. People were far more fascinated with photographs of the exotic won-

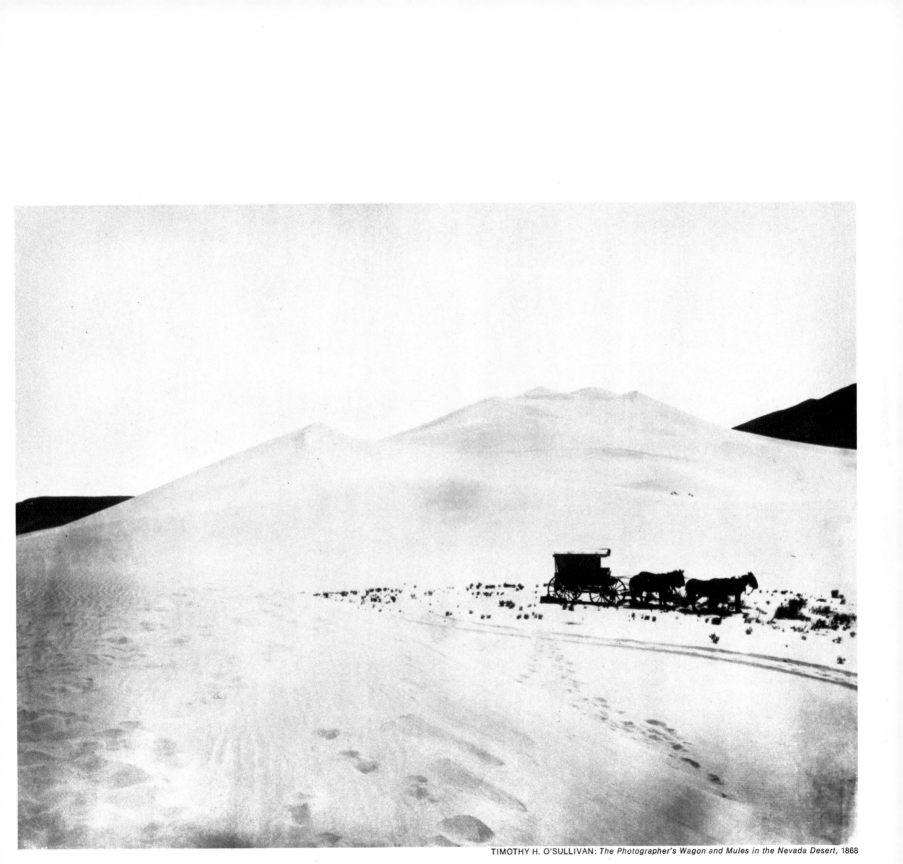

TIMOTHY H. O'SULLIVAN: *The Photographer's Wagon and Mules in the Nevada Desert,* 1868

To capture the lonely vastness of the desert north of Death Valley, Timothy H. O'Sullivan climbed a sand dune and made this picture of the ambulance that served as his photographic van.

ders of the world. True, there had always been artists' drawings that portrayed unfamiliar places. But looking at drawings meant seeing things through another person's eyes and never quite believing them. The camera somehow seemed an extension of one's own vision; a photograph was accepted as real, a faithful image created by a mechanical process.

Through photography, the stay-at-home of the 19th Century could travel by proxy to almost any part of the world. Some of the finest photographers of the era served as his guides. In 1856 Francis Frith, a British photographer and publisher, struggled 600 miles up the Nile to the Second Cataract, bringing back pictures of the Pyramids, the Sphinx and ancient temples along the route *(pages 110-111)*. The Bisson brothers, Louis Auguste and Auguste Rosalie, hauled their equipment to altitudes of 16,000 feet in the French Alps to photograph the peaks, while Carlo Ponti and James Anderson portrayed the watery wonders of Venice and the ruins of ancient Rome.

Strangely enough, one of the most spectacular landscapes of all, on the western frontier of the United States, remained largely unphotographed until the decade following the end of the Civil War. Explorers and artists had been in the Rocky Mountain area long before this time, but the wondrous tales they had told of the region and the sketches they had made were often discounted. Most of these doubts were dispelled when photographers made the western trek. One of the first to go was Timothy H. O'Sullivan, who had worked with Brady before and during the Civil War *(page 98)*.

The hardships and dangers of the Civil War—on two occasions O'Sullivan's camera was toppled by shell fragments while he was taking pictures—proved excellent schooling for his work with government surveying teams in the West. On his first expedition to the Rockies in 1867, the party faced passes blocked with snow drifts of 30 feet or more, capable of swallowing men and mules without a trace. To lessen the hazard, the group moved at night when the bitter cold froze the snow into somewhat firmer footing. One night, O'Sullivan later recounted, 13 grueling hours were required to cross a two-and-a-half mile divide. Hauling mules out of holes in the snow consumed much of the time.

On that same trip, the rapids of the Truckee River in what is now Nevada almost cost O'Sullivan his life. Fortunately he escaped with only a financial loss. The small boat in which he and several other men were traveling was driven off course by the swift current and wedged between two rocks. The men tried to shove off with their oars and succeeded only in losing them. Stripping to his underwear, the photographer dived into the stream to free the boat and was immediately swept under the swirling water. He finally surfaced some distance downstream, managed to swim ashore and yelled to his companions to throw him a line. They did—weighting the end with O'Sul-

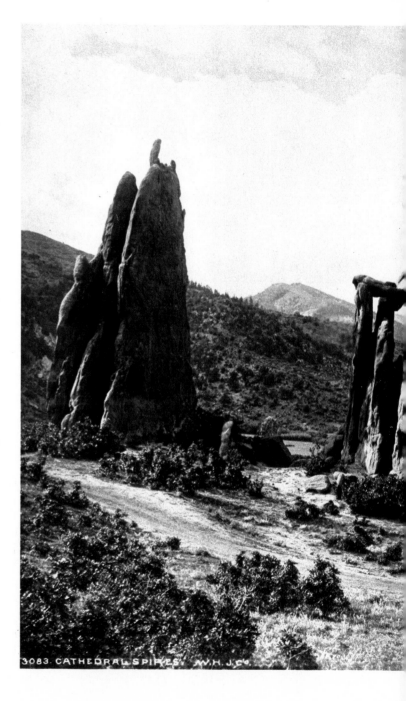

3083. CATHEDRAL SPIRES W.H.J.C°

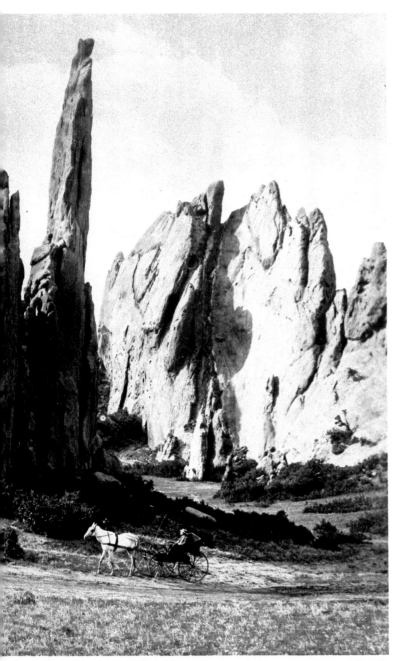

WILLIAM HENRY JACKSON: *Cathedral Spires in the Garden of the Gods, Colorado, 1873*

Views of the American West, like this one of the spectacularly eroded sandstone pinnacles in the foothills of the Rockies, drew streams of tourists when they were seen back East.

livan's purse containing $300 in $20 gold pieces. The line reached O'Sullivan but not the purse, which fell off and disappeared into the water. "I prospected a long time, barefooted, for it," he sadly reported later.

Photographically, O'Sullivan's trip was more successful. He photographed part of the California desert on that first expedition and expressed his fascination with its brilliant mounds of snow-like sand in both pictures *(pages 84-85)* and words. "The contour of the mounds was undulating and graceful," he recalled, "it being continually broken into the sharp edges by the falling away of some of the portions of the mound, which had been undermined by the keen winds that spring up during the last hours of daylight and continue through the night."

O'Sullivan went on five expeditions to the West and brought back some of the finest pictures ever taken of the region. His work, however, attracted little public attention at the time, and when he died, at age 42 of tuberculosis, he was buried in an unmarked grave on Staten Island in New York.

But not all the early photographers who went west were unappreciated. Probably the most celebrated was William Henry Jackson. Born in Keeseville, New York, in 1843, Jackson had become familiar with cameras during his boyhood, thanks to a father who experimented with daguerreotypes. Young Jackson's first interest was painting and at age 15 he left school to earn his living by painting portraits and landscapes and by hand-coloring photographs. Later he went to Vermont and took a steady job as a photographer's assistant. When the Civil War began, he volunteered for the Union Army, served out his enlistment without seeing combat and then returned to Vermont and photography. He was doing well financially but an unhappy love affair caused him to leave in 1866 and he was soon working his way toward the West Coast, part of the time as a "bullwhacker," or driver, with a wagon train. He finally ended up in Omaha running a photographic studio.

Jackson soon became bored with routine studio work, so he fitted out a wagon as a photographic van and set off to take pictures of Indians. It was not an undertaking for a nervous man. The Union Pacific and Central Pacific were then laying tracks westward for the first transcontinental railroad and the Indians around Omaha were forcibly resisting the technological invasion. There were a number of attacks on work crews. But on his first trip, a six-day excursion from Omaha to Cheyenne and back, Jackson managed to persuade local tribesmen not only to leave his scalp in place but to pose for his cameras. The prints sold readily. Encouraged by his success, he took longer journeys and returned with pictures of such sights as the Salt Lake Valley, the Wasatch Mountains and Echo and Weber canyons.

In the summer of 1870, Jackson accompanied Dr. Ferdinand V. Hayden, a geologist and physician, on a United States government survey along the Oregon Trail through Wyoming. This relationship with Hayden was to lead to Jackson's most significant work a year later: pictures that would play a crucial role in preserving for future generations the beauty of the western wilderness. Hayden, fascinated by what he heard in a lecture about the marvels of Yellowstone, persuaded Congress to underwrite an expedition there in 1871; as soon as he had an appropriation to pay a photographer, he recruited Jackson to join the party.

The expedition left Ogden, Utah, in early June. Most of Jackson's photographic gear was transported in a converted ambulance that also served as a darkroom. When Jackson was working in mountainous areas where the wagon could not go, a sturdy mule called "Hypo" assumed the burden and a specially fitted tent became the darkroom. "When hard pressed for time," Jackson reported later, "I had to make a negative in fifteen minutes from the time the first rope was thrown from the pack to the final repacking."

Photographing Yellowstone was a difficult and often risky business, but Jackson was caught up in the excitement of seeing the area for the first time and being the first to record its wonders with a camera. His earlier photographic experience in the wilderness served him well. He was especially adept at what army men refer to as "field expedients," making do with whatever is at hand. When he photographed Mammoth Hot Springs, for example, he employed the subject itself in his photographic processing. After taking and developing his pictures, he used the 120° water that tumbled down the series of semicircular basins to wash the plates, knowing they would dry more quickly because of the heat of the water.

Fortunately, Jackson was a strong man as well as a resourceful one. Once, after taking a number of pictures at the top of Yellowstone's 200-foot Tower Falls, he decided to take some from the bottom without moving all his heavy equipment. He carried only his camera and a few plates, exposed them, climbed back to the summit, developed them, prepared more plates and went down again. To keep the prepared plates moist and sensitive during the ascent and descent, Jackson backed them with wet blotting paper, inserted them in holders, wrapped the holders in a wet towel and then covered the entire package with a black cloth. The first climb down to the bottom and the last up were the most difficult because he had to carry the camera as well as the plates, but the intervening round trips were not easy; four per day was the maximum possible. Even Jackson admitted he paid "a stiff price in labor for one subject."

The results Jackson achieved were worth the effort. He made about 400 negatives of some of the most magnificent scenery on earth. Great canyons, waterfalls, geysers shooting towers of boiling water into the air, placid lakes, lush forests and forbidding sulphur flats—all were part of his photographic

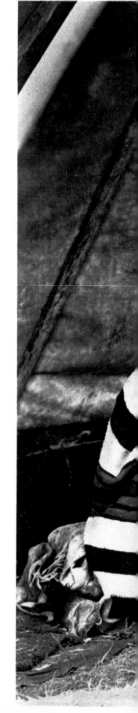

Three Shoshone squaws and a well-wrapped papoose pose for William Henry Jackson's camera inside the entrance to a tepee. In his travels in the West, Jackson took hundreds of such pictures—of Indian tepee villages and pueblos, of men doing tribal dances and women grinding corn, of proud chiefs sitting for their portraits in full-feathered dress. The photographs constitute one of the few authentic records of the American Indians as they lived before they were confined to reservations.

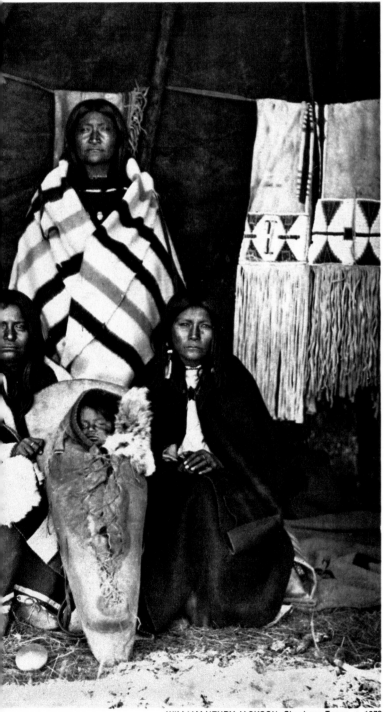

WILLIAM HENRY JACKSON: *Shoshone Tepee, c. 1870*

report. Many of the earlier explorers had been labeled as liars because of the stories they brought back about Yellowstone; Jackson and his cameras provided incontrovertible evidence that the descriptions had been accurate.

Early in the 1871-1872 session in Congress, Senator S. C. Pomeroy of Kansas had introduced a bill calling for the establishment of America's first national park at Yellowstone. Because of the Senate's reluctance to accept the verbal accounts of the area, he had had considerable difficulty in getting consideration of the measure. But the atmosphere changed completely on the day Pomeroy could say to his colleagues, "There are photographs of the valley and of the curiosities, which the senators can see." Once they had seen Jackson's pictures, the Senate and then the House quickly passed the bill and, on March 1, 1872, President Ulysses S. Grant signed it into law. Yellowstone was now set apart "for the benefit and enjoyment of the public." Jackson's photographs, especially his stereoscopic slides, which were sold in great quantities, also helped start Yellowstone's first tourist boom. Wealthy sportsmen, adventurers and even proper Eastern ladies and their families journeyed to the West to see at first hand the sights Jackson had captured with his camera.

During the next six years, Jackson accompanied Hayden on other expeditions, photographing the Grand Tetons in Wyoming, the Rocky Mountains in the Pike's Peak area and the ruins of the pre-Columbian cliff dwellings of the Mesa Verde in Colorado's San Juan mountains. (In 1906 Mesa Verde also became a national park.) After Jackson's job with the United States Geological Survey was eliminated in an economy move in 1878, he struck out on his own and made a modest fortune photographing various parts of the United States, Canada and Mexico. When the halftone printing process came into use in the 1880s he went into the business of engraving photographs for reproduction in newspapers and magazines; once again he prospered. In 1924, at 81, he moved to Washington, D.C., and resumed his career as a painter, which he had never fully given up. When he was 93, he painted a series of oils of the Old West that still hangs in the museum af the Department of the Interior. He maintained his interest in photography until his death in 1942, just months before he would have celebrated his 100th birthday. His name is not likely to be forgotten. Jackson's Canyon along the Oregon-Mormon Trail on the North Platte River, Jackson's Lake in the Grand Teton Mountains and Jackson's Butte in the Mesa Verde are permanent memorials to a great photographer and his work.

In the same decades in which the camera was documenting the events and places of the world, it was also recording the lives of the people of the world. A number of 19th Century photographers made pictures of influential per-

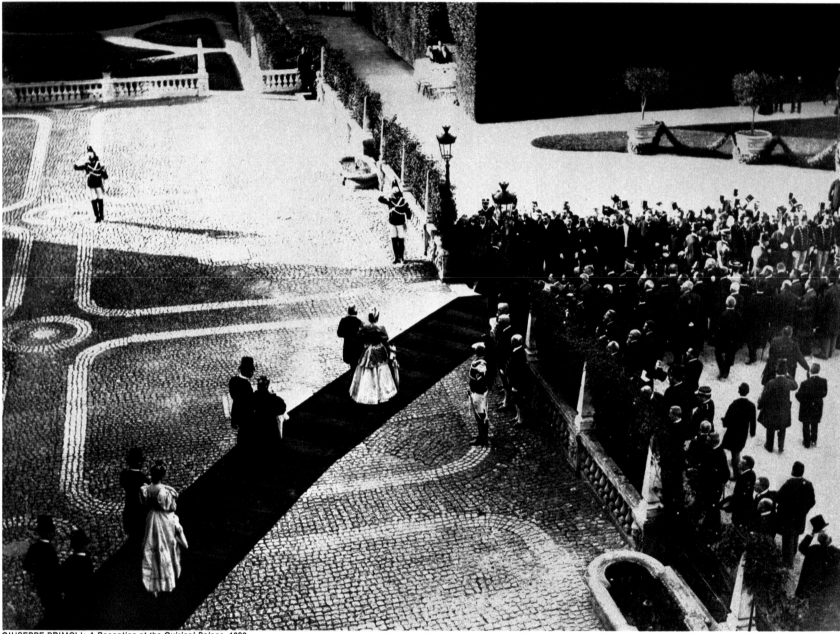

GIUSEPPE PRIMOLI: *A Reception at the Quirinal Palace*, 1893

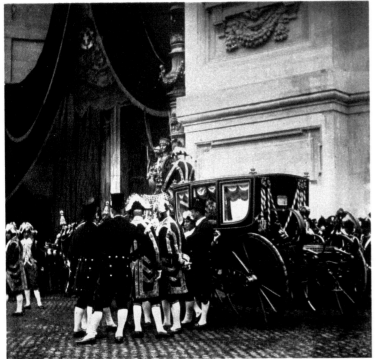

GIUSEPPE PRIMOLI: *Attendants at the Wedding of Vittorio Emanuele III, 1896*

As a member of the European aristocracy, Count Giuseppe Napoleone Primoli had ready access to stylish events. One was the silver wedding anniversary of King Umberto I and Queen Margherita at the King's palace in Rome in 1893, whose grand sweep he captured in the photograph opposite. Another was the wedding of King Vittorio Emanuele III to Princess Helena of Montenegro in 1896, whose fringe details he recorded in the picture above.

sonages that were not portraits intended for private use but were meant to be sold to the public. In 1850 Mathew Brady published *The Gallery of Illustrious Americans,* "containing portraits of twelve of the most eminent citizens of the American Republic since the days of Washington. . . ." The citizens then so eminent included Henry Clay, John James Audubon and Daniel Webster as well as the now half-forgotten President, Millard Fillmore, and midwestern politician Lewis Cass. Brady also photographed all but one of the 20 men who had held the office of President of the United States in the years between 1825 and 1897. (The exception was William Henry Harrison, who died in 1841, before Brady became a practicing photographer.)

Late in the century, Giuseppe Primoli, an Italian count and intimate of the aristocracy of France and Italy, provided an extensive photographic record of the rarefied world of European nobility. His pictures of the upper classes at work and play constitute one of the best single portrayals of the period known as *la Belle Époque (pages 90-93).* Primoli, an extraordinarily energetic man, traveled from one end of Europe to the other, recording its sovereigns attending receptions, riding horseback and in carriages, participating in hunting expeditions and military exercises. He was often followed by a small caravan of servants to help him haul around his collection of cameras, his darkroom equipment and his hundreds of glass plates. Like a modern photojournalist, he was not content until he had exhausted a subject, taking many pictures from different angles, documenting all the details of an event. (It is hardly surprising that in his first three years as a photographer he exposed some 10,000 plates.) And, like a modern reporter, he often sought to reveal a situation not by showing the action itself but by recording people's reactions to it; when he went to a local racetrack, for example, he turned his back on the horses and caught instead the richly changing expressions of the spectators in the stands. Anything and everything interested Primoli. When Buffalo Bill and his road company came to Rome, Primoli was right there, pitching his photographic tent next to those of the Indians and persuading them to allow their pictures to be taken. Yet, enthusiastic as he was about photography, Primoli was no dilettante. He was acutely aware of the realities of life; among his best pictures are photographs that show policemen at work, a woman fixing her hair *(pages 92-93),* even beggars and children sleeping in the streets and prisoners in chains.

Perhaps the most penetrating photographic study of urban life, however, was undertaken by John Thomson in London. He focused on the slums of the British capital and became the first photographer to use pictures deliberately for pointed social comment. His reputation as a photographer was established well before he made London's poor his personal cause. Born in Scotland in 1837, he attended the University of Edinburgh and majored in chemistry, but photography soon became his primary interest. In 1862 he boarded a steamer with his cameras and wet-plate equipment and headed for the Far East. His travels to Siam, Cambodia, Formosa, the Malay Peninsula and China—and his revealing photographs of the peoples, cities and landscapes of those countries—became the basis of a four-volume work, written by Thomson and illustrated with lithographs, of a special type called collotypes, made from his photographs. The books made Thomson one of the best-known photographers in Great Britain.

In the 1870s Thomson met a journalist named Adolphe Smith, who suggested that they collaborate on a book about the London slums. Thomson and Smith were soon at work with camera and notebook. The result was *Street Life in London,* consisting of 36 case histories, each of them illustrated with a Thomson photograph reproduced by a method similar to collotype. The book was published in 1877 and, given its subject matter, the timing could not have been better.

Britain was going through a period of extensive self-examination and social change, a period when, in the words of biographer and critic Lytton Strachey, "Victoria found herself condemned to live in an agitating atmosphere of interminable reform. . . ." One of the troublesome questions being asked has a familiar ring today: Why are so many citizens of a progressive and wealthy society forced to live in abject poverty?

Apparently aware that earlier, nonphotographic treatises on the slums had sometimes been dismissed as hyperbole, Thomson and Smith pointed out in their introduction that they were "bringing to bear the precision of photography in illustration of our subject. The unquestionable accuracy of this testimony will enable us to present true types of the London Poor and shield us from the accusation of either underrating or exaggerating individual peculiarities of appearance."

Thomson did achieve a remarkable balance with his photographs *(pages 94-95).* The filth, the ragged clothes, the dismal surroundings, the degradation and despair are all there, but he also shows that warmth, humor and spirit can continue to flourish even under the worst of conditions. A picture like "The Crawlers"—one of a number of middle-aged women who can barely drag themselves from one place to another—is in itself a photographic essay on the indifference of society. The text comments: "Huddled together on the workhouse steps in Shorts Gardens, these wrecks of humanity, the Crawlers of St. Giles, may be seen both day and night seeking mutual warmth and mutual consolation in their extreme misery. As a rule, they are old women reduced by vice and poverty to that degree of wretchedness which destroys even the energy to beg." The same atmosphere of defeat is also present in other photographs such as "London Nomads," in which two

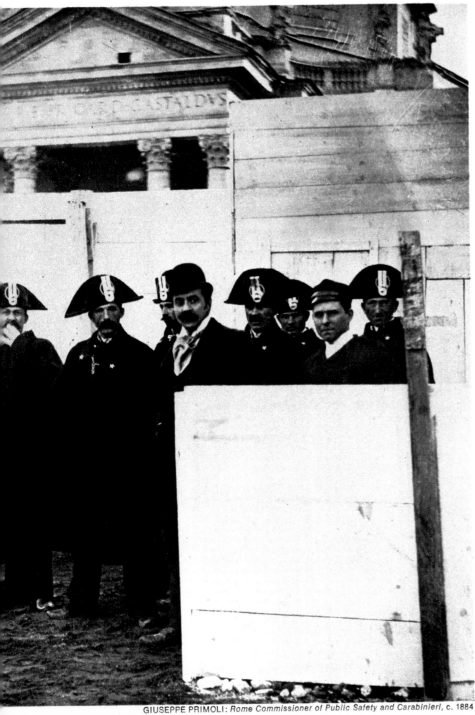

GIUSEPPE PRIMOLI: *Girl Fixing Her Hair,* c. 1895

Like all gifted reporters, Giuseppe Primoli took pains to catch the small, human moments that occur in the lives of ordinary people, such as the policemen at left, posing with their boss amidst barricades set up for a carnival horse race in the streets of Rome, and the girl above, standing on a stool to primp in a mirror while a very attentive admirer looks on.

GIUSEPPE PRIMOLI: *Rome Commissioner of Public Safety and Carabinieri,* c. 1884

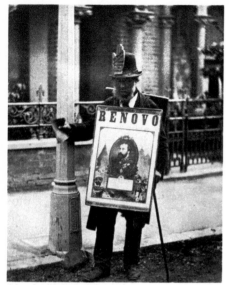
A London "Boardman"

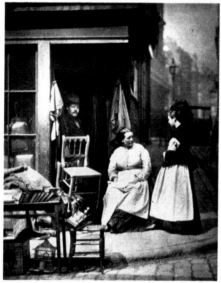
Used Furniture Dealer

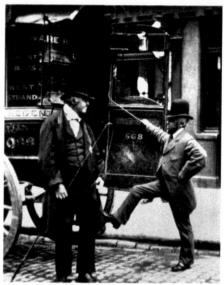
"Cast Iron Billy" (left), an Omnibus Driver

men and two women, dirty, tired and seemingly devoid of interest in anything, are shown outside a battered, gypsy-like wagon, while two children with already aging faces peer out from the wagon's door.

In contrast to such scenes are others of grinning youngsters buying ices from a man with a pushcart, a family posing self-consciously in a park for a street photographer, a young Italian street musician playing a harp for a small but attentive audience. Many of the photographs simply show the day-to-day activities and haunts of the slum dwellers: a second-hand dress shop in which soiled garments hang as limply as sails on an airless sea; a sidewalk "doctor" selling a "cough preventative"; a locksmith working in his street stall; a shoeshine boy; a water cart flushing the streets; a woman buying strawberries from a vendor; boys looking hungrily through the window of a dingy restaurant while the owner stands in the doorway.

In *Street Life in London,* Thomson was doing with his camera what Charles Dickens had done earlier with a number of his novels: assaulting the British conscience with the hope of improving the lot of the poor. The use of photography as an editorial weapon became more and more common in the decades that followed as photographers lashed out at shameful conditions either ignored or treated with apathy by society. In the 1890s, Jacob A. Riis focused on the slums of New York and produced his memorable book of text and pictures, *How the Other Half Lives,* a damning commentary on indifference to poverty in one of the world's richest cities. A decade later, Lewis W. Hine, employing what he called "photo-interpretations," expressed his indignation over the heartless exploitation of child labor in sweatshop factories; his report was a major factor in the passage of child-labor laws in the United States. During the depression of the 1930s, LIFE and FORTUNE photographer Margaret Bourke-White and novelist Erskine Caldwell collaborated on the powerful *You Have Seen Their Faces,* a photographic essay on the bitter human suffering in the South. Today this tradition of photographic reportage and commentary has become an integral part of modern communications and a major force behind communal action, from the newspaper story on alienated youth to the magazine picture essay on environmental pollution. ☐

The first known use of photography as a tool of social commentary was a book called "Street Life in London," published in 1877, a collection of essays, as the preface put it, on the "various means by which our unfortunate fellow-creatures endeavour to earn, beg or steal their daily bread." The photographs, some of which are shown here, were taken by John Thomson, who had established a reputation with perceptive portraits as well as with several books of photographs recording Far Eastern cultures. "Street Life" was sold on London newsstands in 12 installments of three photographs and essays each, and added to the growing awareness of urban poverty.

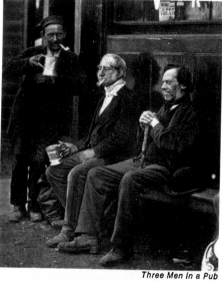
Three Men in a Pub

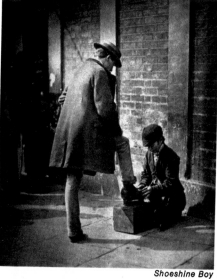
Shoeshine Boy

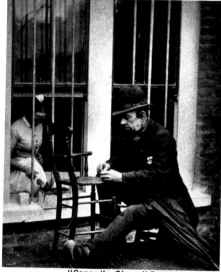
"Caney the Clown," Recaning a Chair

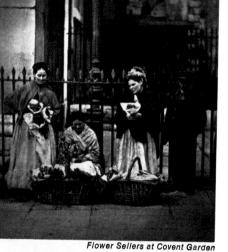
Flower Sellers at Covent Garden

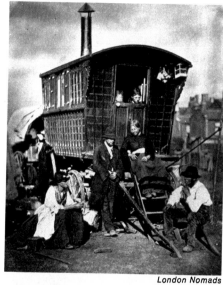
London Nomads

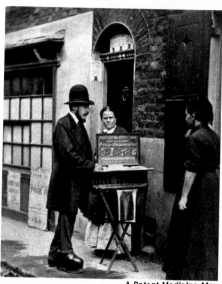
A Patent-Medicine Man

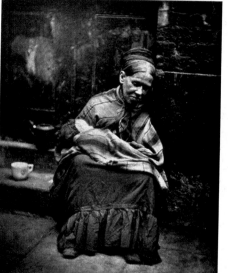
One of the "Crawlers," Minding a Child

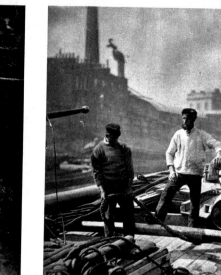
Bargemen on the Thames

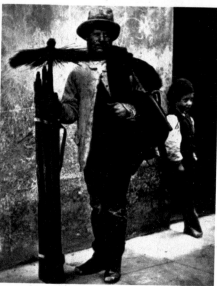
Chimney Sweep

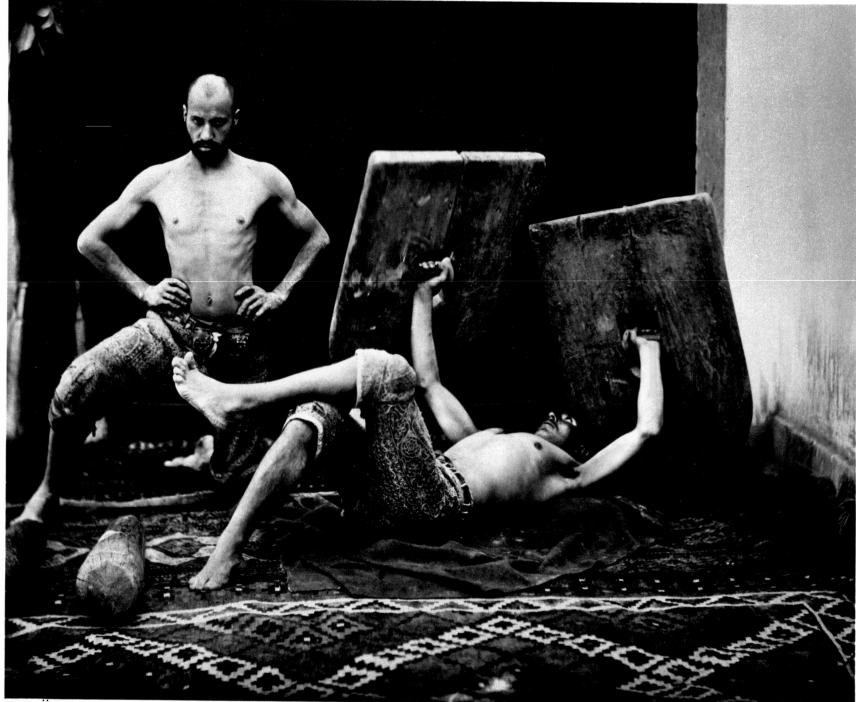

ERNST HÖLTZER: *Persian Gymnasts*, c. 1880

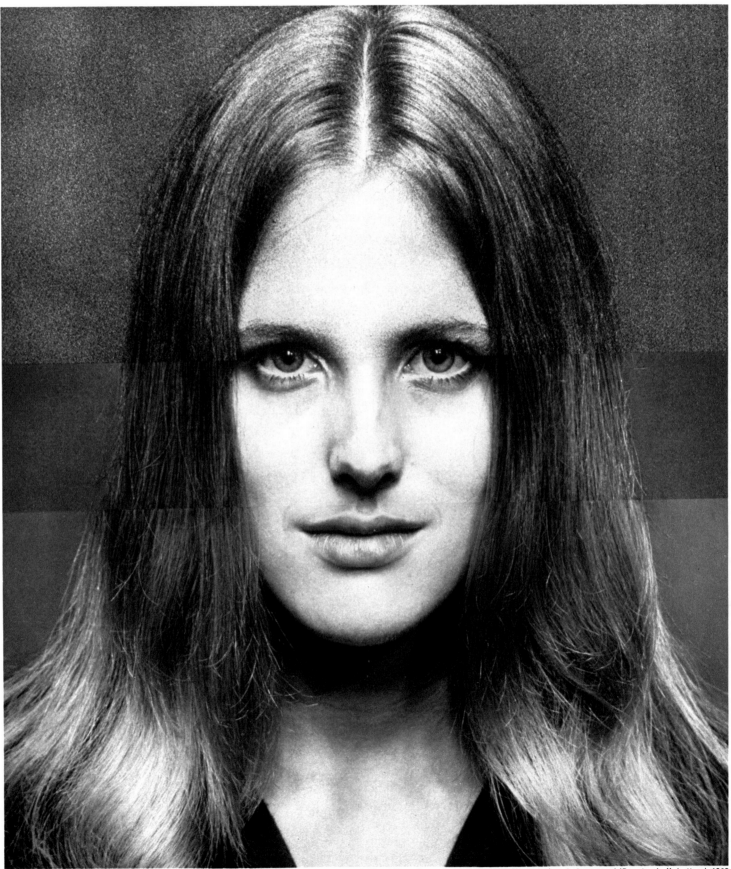

EVELYN HOFER: *Composite portrait, using films of high speed (Royal-X, top), medium speed (Plus-X, center) and slow speed (Panatomic-X, bottom), 1969*

How Film Works

For photography, the advances in light-sensitive materials in the later years of the 19th Century were equivalent in impact to the effect of the automobile on the rest of civilization. Certainly the leap from clumsy plates to easily handled, factory prepared rolls of film was as great as the leap from horses to cars—and film pioneer George Eastman, like Henry Ford, saw to it that millions of Americans got aboard in a hurry. The first films were as cantankerous and slow as the early horseless carriages, balking whenever photographers attempted to capture a dimly lighted or fast-moving subject, but technology soon remedied that. Today, in terms of sensitivity, resolution of detail and other yardsticks of performance, modern films can run tight circles around their forebears.

Modern films operate on the same basic principles as the late 19th Century products. Light is captured by microscopic crystals of a compound called silver bromide (usually containing a trace of silver iodide). The crystals are carried in a transparent gelatin made from animal hides and bones, and this mixture, called an emulsion, is thinly spread on a plastic base that provides support. While these features have been around a long time, today's films are vastly more effective at registering light than earlier versions. For years manufacturers could not figure out why batches of film, all containing the same type of silver bromide crystals, showed wide differences in sensitivity. The secret seemed to be in the gelatin that held the crystals; it finally became apparent that the ability of film to record light depended on, of all things, the diet of the animals whose hides went into the gelatin. The hides of cattle that ate mustard plants produced much more sensitive film than those from cattle raised on other diets. In 1925 scientists discovered that the key ingredient contributed by the diet was a sulphur-containing oil from the mustard plants. Since then manufacturers have learned that there are many other compounds that affect sensitivity of films. Today, these are synthesized and added to the emulsion in carefully metered amounts to make batches of film of uniform sensitivity.

Another factor which affects a film's sensitivity is the size of its silver bromide crystals. An emulsion containing large crystals needs less light to form an image than an emulsion with small crystals. On the face of it, since high sensitivity is always desirable in photography, it might seem sensible for manufacturers to produce nothing but large-crystal emulsions. Unfortunately, there is a drawback: the bigger the crystals are, the poorer the image. A very sensitive, coarse-crystal emulsion will produce a grainy picture, speckled and lacking in fine detail. So, manufacturers offer a choice. A photographer can select a very sensitive but grainy film, a very fine-grained but less sensitive film, or a compromise between the two. It is not yet possible to have the best of both worlds, but some films come close to that ideal, combining great sensitivity with remarkable freedom from graininess. Today manufacturers have become so skillful at controlling the size of silver bromide crystals that they can now design a film with just the sort of characteristics they desire.

The usual way of describing a film is by its sensitivity or speed, indicated by its ASA rating—the numerical system, devised by the American Standards Association, that grades film according to the amount of light needed to produce a normal image. Higher numbers mean that a photographer can get his picture with less illumination (or can use a higher shutter speed to stop action). For convenience' sake, photographic equipment dealers often refer to films as being slow, medium or fast—slow being in the ASA 20 to 50 range, medium in the 100 to 200 range and fast in the 400 to 1250 range.

Photographers, quite naturally, crave simplicity and often rely on a single kind of medium-speed or fast film for all their pictures. One type may be insufficient, but just two—a slow, fine-grain one and a fast one—will do justice to almost any scene. It is frequently unwise to choose a fast film when it is not necessary to stop action or handle dim light, for a slow film usually yields a sharper, less grainy picture. The differences can be very significant indeed.

There is more to consider in selecting a film than simply its speed and graininess, of course. Some films are more sensitive to certain colors than others are. Early films recorded only the shorter wavelengths of light; modern films contain dyes to sensitize the silver bromide crystals to long wavelengths as well. They record the entire visible spectrum, although how closely they match human perception of the way the spectrum ought to look in black and white may vary from film to film. Some types can even be sensitized to very long waves the eye cannot see. And the instant-developing film of the Polaroid process provides unique effects of its own.

Film technology has come a long way. Sensitivity has been vastly increased, graininess reduced, and color-response broadened to include the whole visible spectrum. And many lesser problems of earlier films have been solved: for example, today's films contain dyes that prevent haloes from forming around highlights of a picture. Despite all these advances, the manufacturers may soon have to deal with a brand new set of problems, for radical types of film are in the offing. Since silver is becoming scarcer and more expensive, laboratories around the world are trying to find a means of recording images without silver compounds. Scientists hope to refine the quality of the electrostatic printing process—used in office copiers —enough so that it can provide the realistic images needed for photography. Other scientists speak optimistically of films that substitute nitrogen bubbles for silver in forming an image. Some sort of change is certainly coming, but the films of today will not be easy to surpass.

Making an Image in Silver

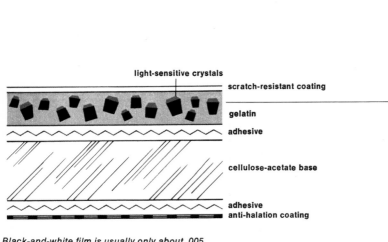

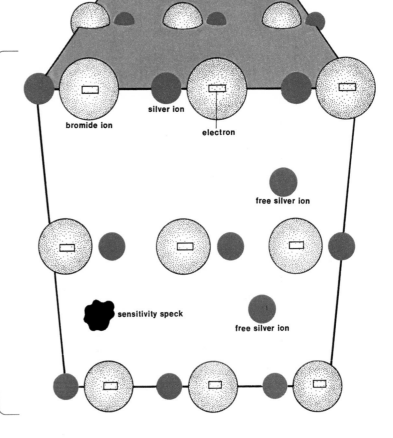

Black-and-white film is usually only about .005 inch thick, but it is made up of a number of layers, as shown above, each serving a specific purpose. The surface consists of a thin protective coating to prevent scratches on the emulsion layer below. This emulsion layer—the crucial region where the image is formed—consists of about 60 per cent gelatin and 40 per cent light-sensitive crystals. Beneath the emulsion is an adhesive substance which binds it to the next layer. The thickest layer is the film base, a firm but flexible plastic, which provides support. The base is backed, by means of another adhesive bond, with an anti-halation coating, which prevents light from reflecting back through the emulsion to cause haloes around bright parts of the picture.

The process that creates a picture on a piece of film involves a remarkable reaction between light and the crystals spread through the gelatin of the emulsion layer. According to current theory, the reaction can be set off when one crystal—only about 40 millionths of an inch across—is struck by as few as two photons of light (a flashlight bulb emits a million billion photons per second). Each crystal is made up of silver and bromine; in the crystal their atoms are electrically charged—that is, they are ions that are held together in a cubical arrangement by electrical attraction. If a crystal were really a perfect structure lacking any irregularities, it would not react to light. However, a number of the silver ions in the average crystal are out of place in the structure and these are free to move about to help form an im-

age. The crystal also contains impurities—such as molecules of silver sulfide—that play a crucial role in the trapping of light energy.

As indicated by the diagrams on the opposite page, an impurity—called a sensitivity speck—and the out-of-place silver ions work together to build a small collection of uncharged atoms of silver metal when the crystal is struck by light. This bit of metallic silver, built up with the aid of light energy, is the beginning of what is known as the latent image; it is too small to be visible under even the most powerful microscope. But when developing chemicals go to work, they use the latent image specks of metallic silver in an exposed crystal as a sort of hook to which the rest of the silver in the crystal becomes attached, forming the image.

A silver bromide crystal (above) has a cubic structure somewhat like a jungle gym, in which silver (small black balls) and bromine (larger white balls) are held in place by electrical attraction. Both are in the form of ions—atoms possessing electrical charge. Each bromide ion has an extra electron (small box)—that is, one more electron than an uncharged bromine atom does, giving it a negative charge; each silver ion has one electron less than an uncharged silver atom does and is positively charged. The irregularly shaped object in the crystal represents a "sensitivity speck." In actuality, each crystal possesses many such specks, or imperfections, which are essential to the image-forming process (shown schematically at right).

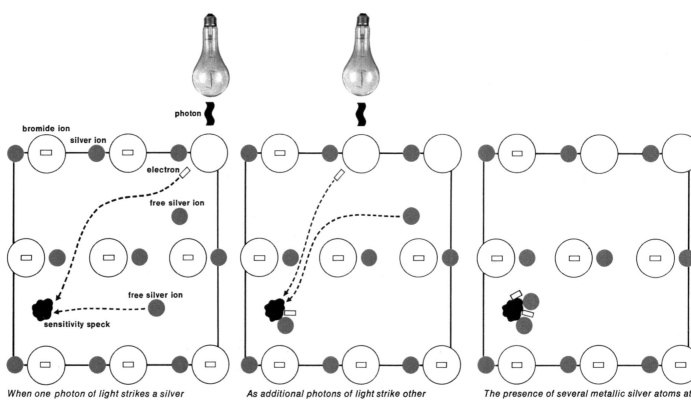

photon

bromide ion

silver ion

electron

free silver ion

free silver ion

sensitivity speck

When one photon of light strikes a silver bromide crystal, image formation begins. The photon gives its energy to a bromide ion's extra electron, lifting it to a higher energy level. Then the negatively charged electron can roam the structure of the crystal until it reaches a sensitivity speck. There, its electrical attraction pulls a positively charged free silver ion to it.

As additional photons of light strike other bromide ions in the crystal and release electrons, more silver migrates to the sensitivity speck. The electrons join up with the silver ions, balancing their electrical charges and making them atoms of silver metal. However, if the crystal were examined through a microscope at this stage, no change would be discernible.

The presence of several metallic silver atoms at a sensitivity speck constitutes a latent image —an invisible chemical site that will serve as the starting point for the conversion of the whole crystal to silver during development. The developer enormously magnifies the slight chemical change caused by light energy and creates the visible photographic image.

A negative is formed when millions of exposed crystals are converted to silver metal by the developer. The result is a record of the camera's view in which the film areas struck by the most light are darkened by metallic silver, while the areas struck by no light remain transparent after processing, since they contain no silver. The intermediate areas have varying amounts of silver, creating shades of gray that depend not only on the amount of light striking the film but also on the color of the light, the type of film and the way it was exposed in the camera.

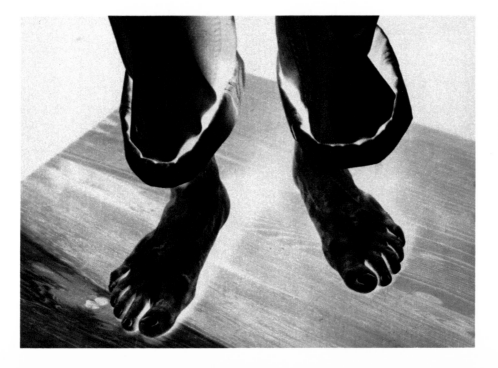

The Polaroid Land Process

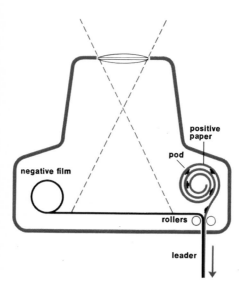

Some Polaroid Land cameras are loaded with two separate spools containing negative film and positive printing paper attached to a single leader. The negative is exposed simply by pressing the shutter, as in an ordinary camera. The leader is then pulled, drawing both negative and positive through a pair of steel rollers and out of the camera. The compression by the steel rollers ruptures a pod of jellylike chemicals attached to the positive paper, initiating development inside the sandwich. After 10 seconds or so, the positive is peeled away from the negative, revealing a finished picture.

When Edwin Land announced his first picture-in-a-minute camera in 1947, a major photographic equipment dealer dismissed it as a gimmick that would not last. Few predictions have ever been farther off the mark. Twenty years later, as many as 14 million Americans owned Polaroid Land cameras and the Polaroid Corporation was the second largest maker of photographic products in the nation. The "gimmick" had been refined to turn out high-quality pictures in only 10 to 20 seconds by taking advantage of a unique processing technique.

In the ordinary photographic process, film is exposed in the camera and later developed to produce a negative. Positive prints are then made in the darkroom by projecting light through this negative and exposing a second emulsion—the light-sensitive printing paper—which then must be developed. Polaroid Land film, however, provides both a negative emulsion and positive paper in one package. After the picture is snapped, the negative and positive are tightly sandwiched together. The image is transferred from one to the other by chemicals at the center of the sandwich, rather than by light. The positive image is formed with the aid of silver from the *unexposed* crystals of the negative—which would simply be washed away during the development of an ordinary film.

The way the camera makes a positive-negative sandwich is shown on this page and the chemical transfer of the image is illustrated opposite. In essence, the Polaroid Land process creates a highly efficient darkroom that is held in the hand for a few seconds, then thrown away when the work is done.

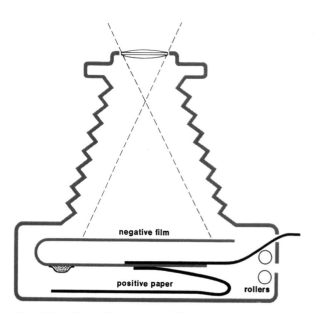

Most Polaroid Land film comes in pack form for easy loading. The pack consists of a box containing flat sheets of negative and positive materials, and is simply snapped into the back of the camera. First, the picture is exposed (above). The negative will then have to be turned upside down to meet properly with the positive paper. The photographer does this by simply pulling on a white tab (below).

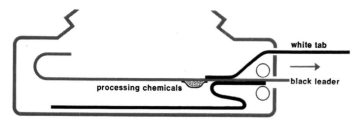

When the white tab is pulled, the exposed negative turns upside down and is brought close to the steel rollers (the positive paper has not yet moved). Next, a black leader is pulled, drawing both the negative and the positive through the rollers and breaking the pod of chemicals in the process (below). The chemicals are thus spread evenly within the sandwich to develop and fix the picture.

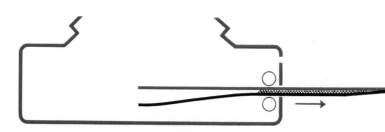

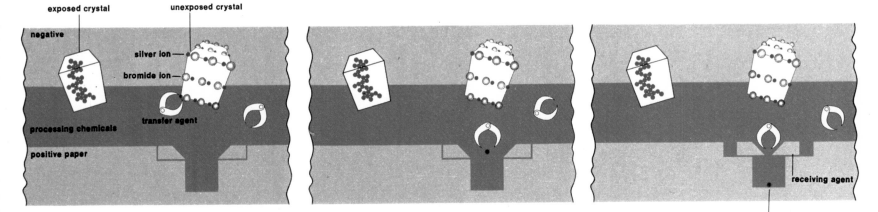

When Polaroid Land film is developed, exposed crystals in the negative are reduced to silver metal in the usual fashion. But the processing solution also contains a transfer agent that acts on unexposed crystals. This transfer agent, *represented by pincers above, latches onto the silver ions in an unexposed crystal.*

After a silver ion is snatched away from an unexposed crystal in the negative emulsion, the transfer agent carries it to the positive side of the sandwich. Because the distance from the negative to the positive paper is only about .0002 inch, the silver ion travels directly across the gap, with very little sideways motion.

On the surface of the positive paper is a receiving agent, represented by a pair of sliding trapdoors, which acts as a catalyst and takes the ionic silver from the transfer agent—and at the same time changes the silver to its metallic form. The build-up of millions of silver atoms, in this way, forms a positive image.

Polaroid's Virtue: Speed without Graininess

The performance of Polaroid Land films is as unusual as their chemical means of making an image. While ordinary films generally suffer in graininess if they are fast, the Polaroid Land films do not. This behavior is demonstrated by the pictures at right, taken with Polaroid Land films rated at ASA 50, ASA 400 and ASA 3000. The main reason for the lack of graininess in all three of these pictures is the extremely narrow gap at the center of the positive-negative film sandwich that produces the Polaroid Land photograph. This permits the silver ions to travel in a straight line from the negative to the positive surface and they are less likely to form random clumps of silver, which are the chief cause of graininess and loss of detail.

Among Polaroid Land films, the ASA 50 film is unique in that it provides the photographer with a negative as well as a positive. (With all the other Polaroid Land films, the negative is always thrown away.) However, the negative is subject to the same laws of development that operate with ordinary films —that is, its graininess will increase with speed. Therefore, this film *must* be slow in order to yield a negative that will have a desirably fine grain.   □

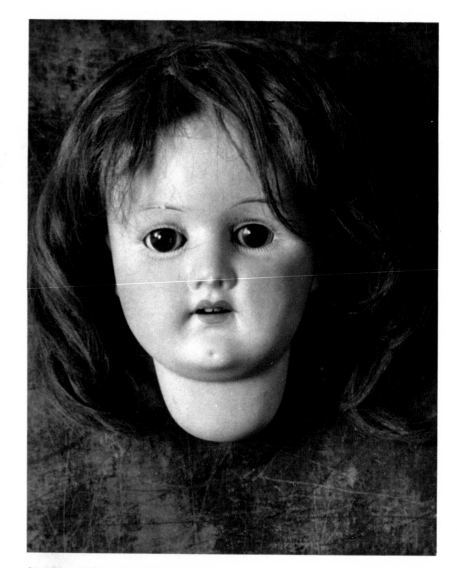

Slow ASA 50 Polaroid Land film produces grain-free pictures in 20 seconds—and also provides the photographer with a usable negative from which an enlargement, as much as 25 times original size, can be made. Other Polaroid Land films can be enlarged only by rephotographing the positive print with a camera to obtain a printable negative.

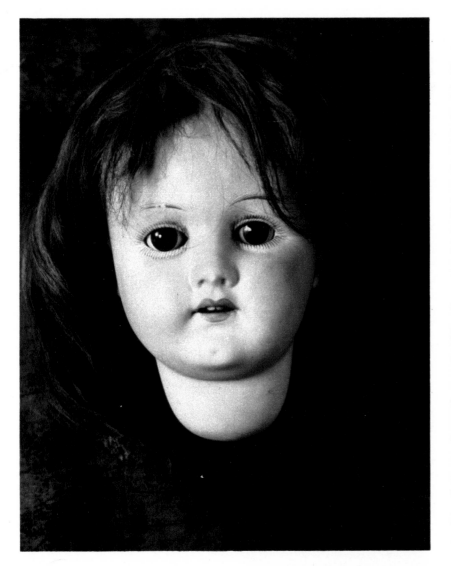

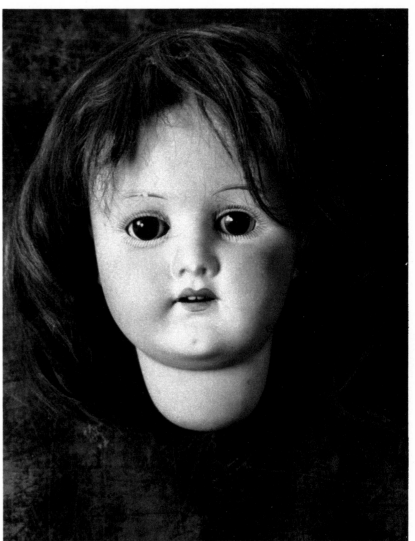

Medium-speed ASA 400 Polaroid Land film also produces a virtually grain-free image in 15 seconds. It is a good choice for general purpose photography. In addition, many professionals use this film for exposure testing, taking preliminary Polaroid pictures of a subject to make sure that the lighting effect is what they desire, before shooting with ordinary film.

The extraordinarily fast ASA 3000 Polaroid Land film is remarkable not only for its great speed but for the fact that such speed is achieved without sacrificing grain quality. It is the most widely used of all the Polaroid Land films. It produces a 4 x 5 positive print in 15 seconds at room temperature; a longer development time is needed to get a good image in cold weather.

Fitting the Film to the Picture

Many camera stores stock a wide variety of black-and-white films ranging from very slow ASA 20 to superfast ASA 1250. Since faster films produce grainier pictures, a photographer will theoretically get optimum results by selecting the slowest film that suits each lighting situation.

In practice, however, it is inconvenient and unnecessary to work with a dozen types of film. Of the three general speed categories—slow, medium and fast—many photographers use a moderately fast film, such as ASA 400, for almost all of their work. This is possible because film manufacturers have made great strides toward reducing the grain problem in such high quality, fast films as Kodak Tri-X, Ilford HP4, GAF Super Hypan and Agfa Isopan-Ultra.

The portrait of actor Kirk Douglas opposite reveals the precision of detail, unmarred by grain, that can be obtained with a fast film—in this case, Tri-X. The picture was taken with a Hasselblad camera by Jeanloup Sieff, a French photographer best known for his fashion illustrations. Stopping down his aperture to f/16 at 1/60 second, he employed electronic flash to add brilliance to the highlights of the actor's face. The result was an extraordinarily intense close-up view in which every pore and whisker is sharply revealed.

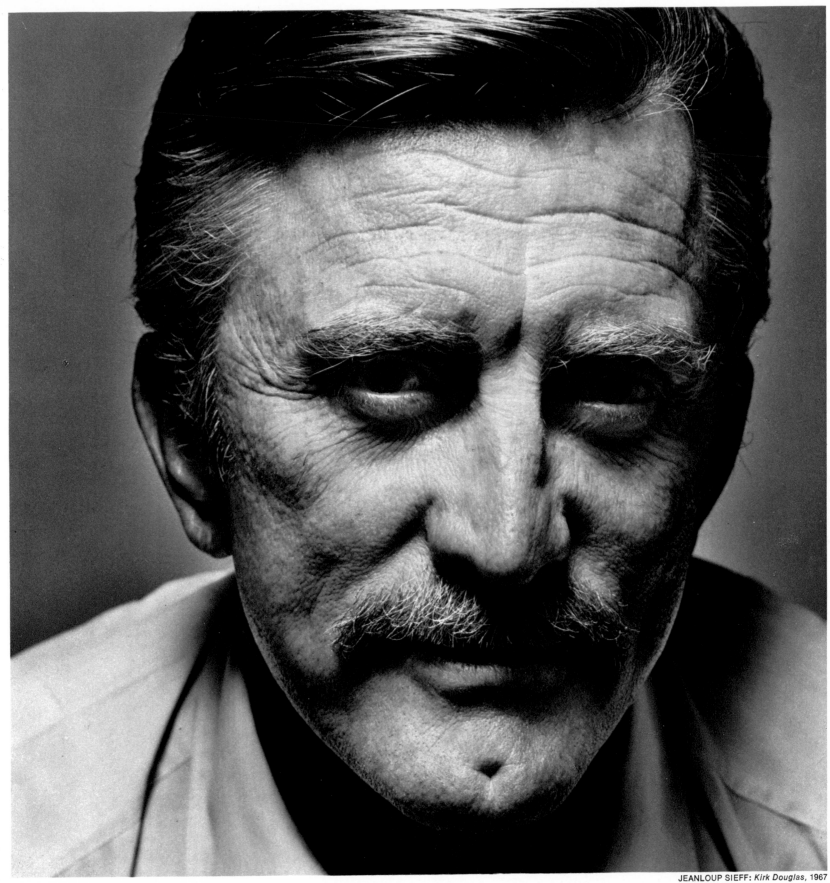

JEANLOUP SIEFF: *Kirk Douglas*, 1967

139

When Speed is Essential

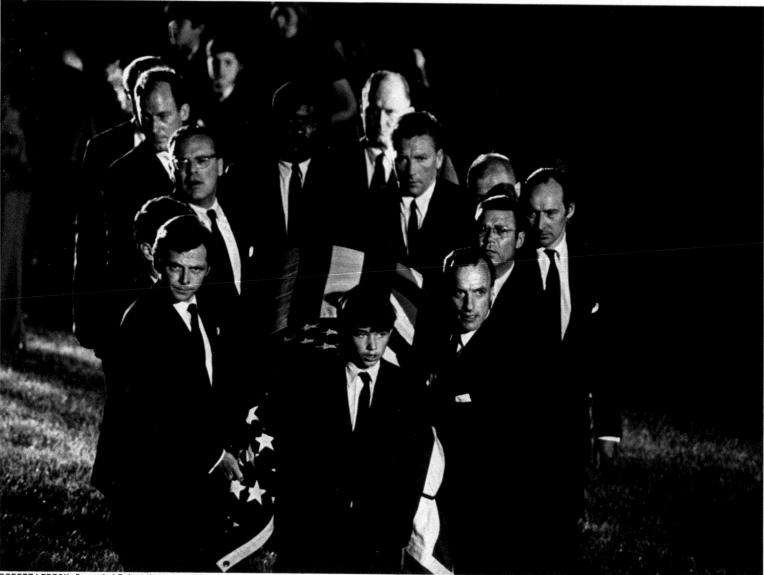

ROBERT LEBECK: *Funeral of Robert Kennedy,* 1968

Modern fast films not only yield sharp, detailed images, but do this with light that only a few years ago would have seemed hopelessly dim. Even if pushed beyond normal limits and given a good deal less light than the standard ASA

number calls for, these films can still produce a good image. German photo-journalist Robert Lebeck exploited this trait of fast film when he photographed the funeral of Senator Robert F. Kennedy at Arlington National Cemetery in

June of 1968. Using a 300mm lens set wide open and a shutter speed of 1/16 second, he exposed his Tri-X as if it were rated at ASA 1000 instead of the normal ASA 400 rating. In the solemn scene above, the pallbearers carrying

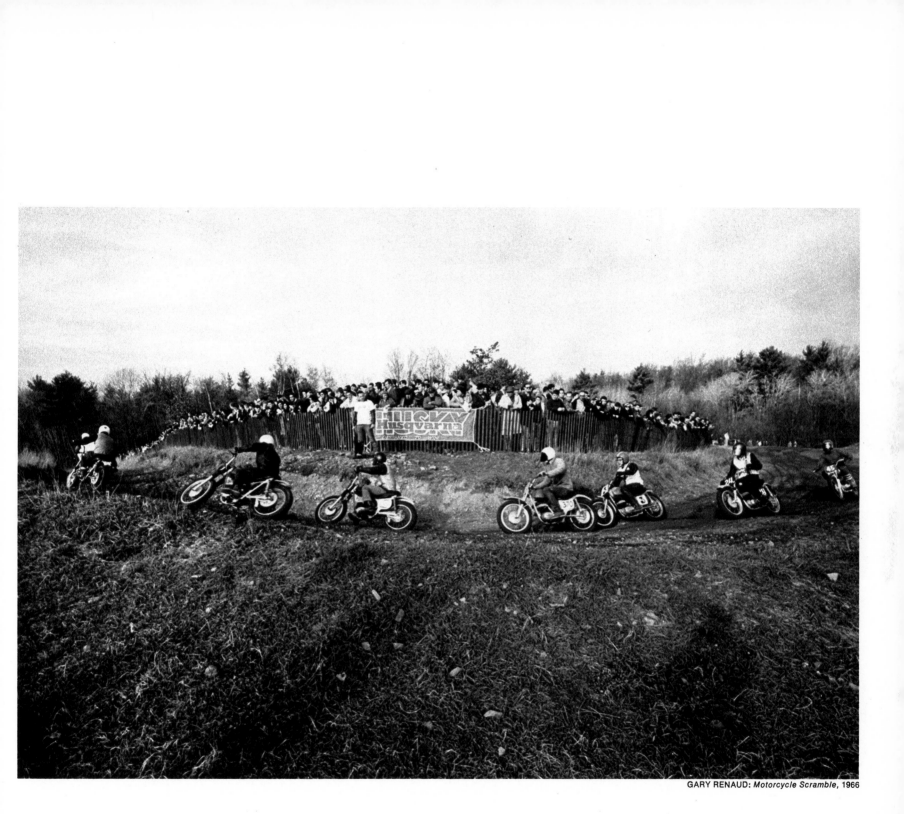

GARY RENAUD: *Motorcycle Scramble,* 1966

the flag-draped coffin are led by Senator Kennedy's son, Robert F. Jr.

With fast films' ability to cope with dim light goes their natural ability to stop rapid motion. When Gary Renaud took his picture of a motorcycle race at a dirt track in Pepperell, Massachusetts *(above),* he had to set his shutter at 1/500 second to freeze the swift action of the racers careening around the course. But the speed of his film—combined with the sunlight of a bright day—enabled him to set his aperture at f/11 for great depth of field. As a result of the small f-stop, even the grass in the foreground and the audience in the background of the picture are as sharply defined as his fast-moving subjects.

Making an Asset of Graininess

Certain photographs gain a misty, almost dreamlike beauty when rendered with a grainy texture. Fast films lend themselves to this effect more readily than slow ones because of the larger size of their silver bromide crystals. (However, any film will produce grainy images if it is suitably manipulated when it is developed.)

William Klein selected a fast film to create this grainy picture of workmen changing a street lamp near a Russian Orthodox church in Moscow. He shot the picture with a 300mm lens on a Pentax and intentionally overexposed it.

Overexposing a negative increases the amount of metallic silver in the negative and makes graininess more visible; it also allows the light to penetrate deeper into the emulsion, where it bounces erratically off crystals and further increases graininess. The combination of overexposure and enlargement of a 35mm negative produced a photograph with very coarse texture. Transformed in this manner, the clustered turrets, crosses and ornate lamp-fixtures of the scene become tantalizing echoes of the past seeming to reach the viewer across a wide gulf of time.

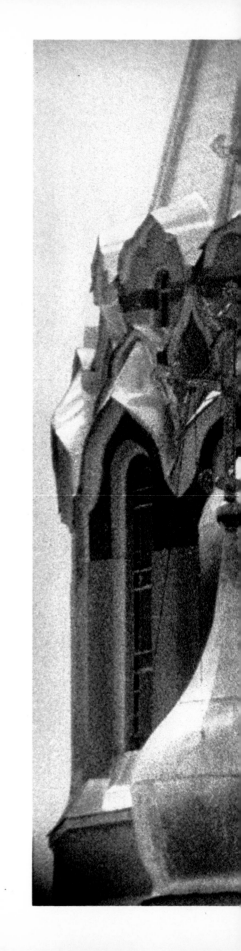

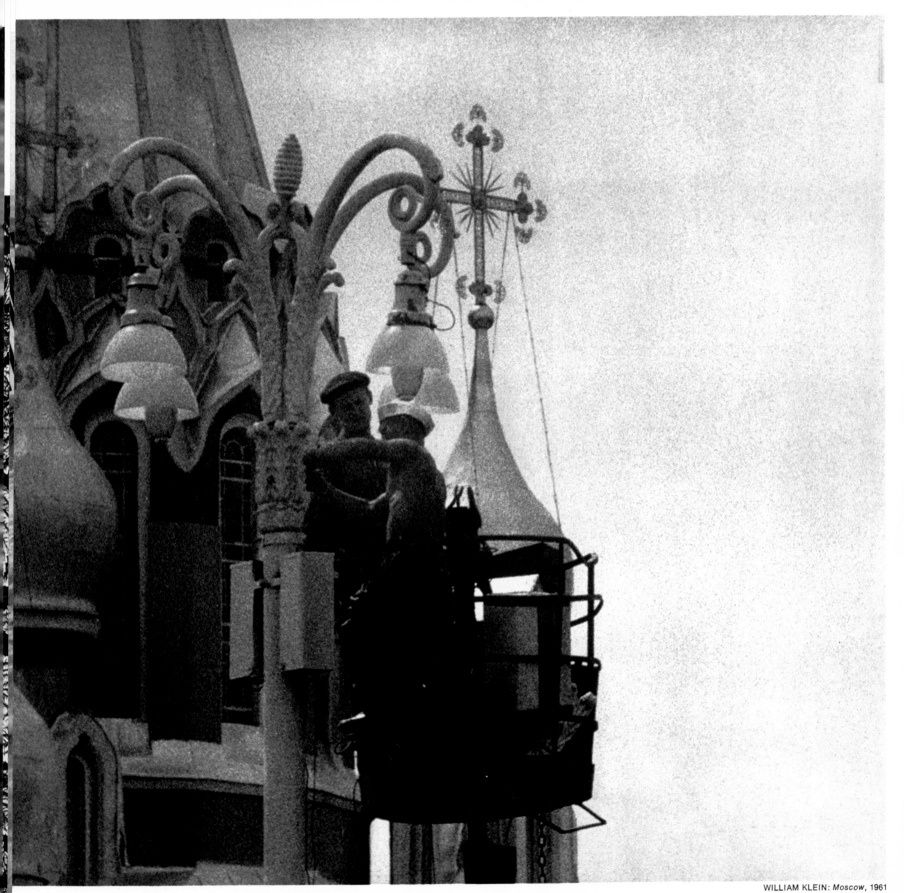

WILLIAM KLEIN: *Moscow,* 1961

143

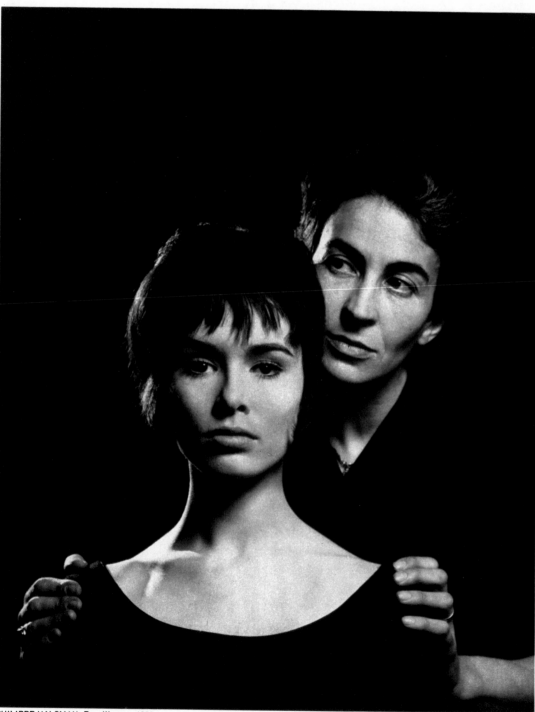

PHILIPPE HALSMAN: *Two Women*, 1958

Exposure: Key to Image Quality 5

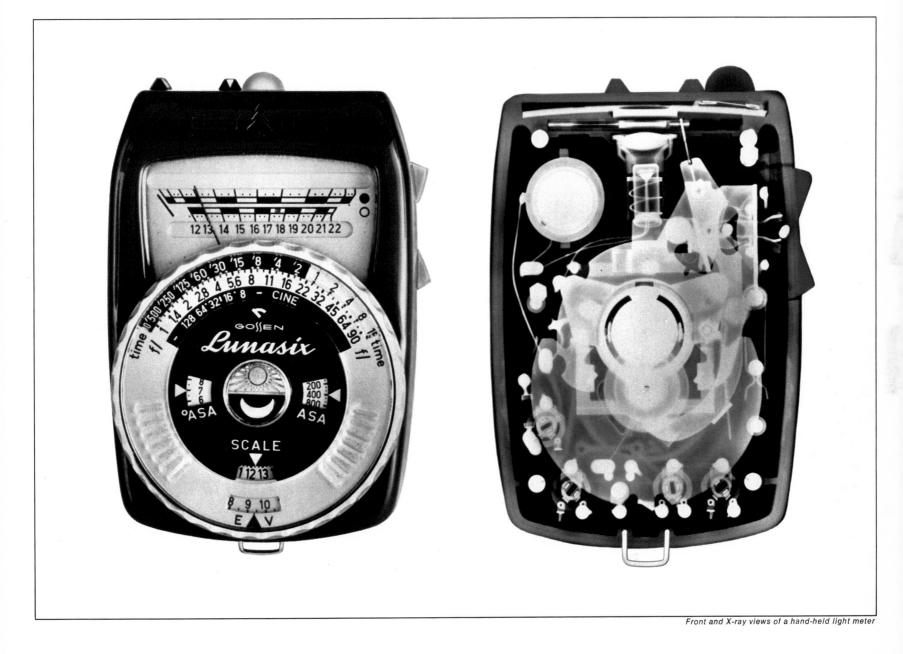

Front and X-ray views of a hand-held light meter

How to Expose for a Good Negative

In the early days of photography, there was a brief period when a photographer could see exactly how his picture was coming out at the time he was taking it. He simply watched the plate through a hole in the camera and, when a good image had been recorded, he stopped the exposure. Some professionals still determine the exposure needed for a good negative by the direct method of making test pictures (conveniently done with a camera adapted for Polaroid Land film). But most photographers rely on light meters and judgment. With films of standardized sensitivity, and with versatile meters to gauge light intensity, an experienced photographer can be almost as certain of getting the negative he wants as his 19th Century counterpart was when he actually observed the image forming inside the camera.

Setting the exposure is the final step—after film has been chosen and lighting is fixed—that determines how a scene will be recorded. In front of the camera is a world of rich and subtle colors, of a variety of textures, of strong and diffuse light—all to be translated, on black-and-white film, into tones of gray. The colors, of course, are lost. But with filters it is possible to control the exposure of black-and-white film to individual colors so that they can be distinguished one from another by differences in their shades of gray. Clouds can be made lighter than the blue sky, red apples a bit darker than green leaves, duplicating in gray tones the relative contrasts that color makes in nature.

But a photograph has only a limited number, or zones, of gray; at best, the brightest areas it records will seem 50 times brighter than the deepest black. Nature is far less limited. In an ordinary scene, some areas may be 200 times brighter than others, and the eye readily detects the detailed features in the darkest as well as the brightest regions. The photograph must compress this great range, and in doing so some details will be lost as the fine distinctions between slightly differing tones of gray merge into one. Which details are lost and which registered depends mainly on exposure.

Adjusting exposure for maximum detail is, to most photographers, the way to get a technically good negative. The explanation is simple: Undesirable details can be suppressed fairly easily later, during the printing process, but no darkroom legerdemain can supply details that are missing from the negative. To achieve maximum detail, the rule of thumb is: Expose for the shadows. That way the scene's darkest important features, reflecting the least light and producing the least silver metal in the developed image, are certain to be recorded rather than omitted entirely. Bright areas may then be so strongly registered that those portions of the negative seem blank patches of solid silver; rarely, however, are these overexposed sections as featureless as they appear, and much of their detail can be brought out in the final print by a number of darkroom techniques. Thus overexposure, while undesirable, is seldom as serious a defect as underexposure, and the time-honored exhortation "expose for the shadows" remains useful guidance. Also it should be remembered that most modern film has a considerable tolerance for overexposure. If the aperture is a stop or two greater than lighting conditions require, or the shutter speed is somewhat slower, the results are rarely disastrous. In most instances, the miscalculation can be easily remedied in the printing.

When time and circumstances permit, many photographers make certain of getting at least one optimum negative by "bracketing." One picture is taken at the apparently correct exposure, a second is made at one f-stop greater than the first and a third at one f-stop less. When he is ready to print, the photographer can select the negative that will give him the greatest tonal range in the finished photograph.

Getting a properly exposed negative is much easier now that photoelectric meters can be used to "take a reading" of the light falling on or reflected by the subject. Many different kinds of meters are now available, either as separate instruments or built into the camera. Meters vary, of course, in their degree of accuracy and in their ability to read low-level light, but almost any reasonably good meter will serve under normal conditions. For unusually difficult circumstances, specialized types are available. All measure light by the electrical reaction it causes when it strikes certain sensitive materials. Some built-in meters are interconnected to the camera's shutter and aperture, adjusting them automatically for the exposure without intervention by the photographer. More useful, however, are those—built-in or separate—that indicate their light measurements with pointers and scales, permitting the photographer to apply his own judgment as he interprets the reading.

Judgment is still necessary, even with the most accurate meter. For one thing, the area in the scene gauged by the meter may not be the one that is most important to the picture; the reading can then indicate an exposure that seems technically correct yet fails to produce a negative with detail where it counts. And for the finest results, the film's limited range of response to light must also be taken into account. Most scenes contain interesting details in many areas of widely varying brightness. The photographer must decide which are the most important and adjust his exposure accordingly; he may choose to forego the features in some dark sections in order to be certain of natural rendition of those in very bright sections—or vice versa. Only by careful study of the lights and darks in a scene can a photographer interpret exposure meter readings to get the kind of negative that will produce a good print: one with a full range of tones from pure blacks to pure whites, with a great many distinct zones of gray between the extremes, and with sharply defined detail in nearly all those zones. □

Light Meters and How to Use Them

The most important piece of equipment for any photographer who wants consistently accurate exposures is a good light, or exposure, meter. Light meters come in several basic varieties: self-contained instruments that are held in the hand; clip-on kinds that attach to a camera, and meters that are built into the camera itself. The built-in kinds are becoming more and more popular because they are so convenient. Yet many photographers, especially professionals, prefer the separate hand-held instruments, particularly when they want very precise control over pictures—for example, in doing portrait or architectural photography, when it may be necessary to set up a camera on a tripod and then be free to approach various parts of the scene and take light readings from close up.

The photoelectric light meters made today operate on one or the other of two light-sensing systems. The simpler ones employ selenium cells, which convert the energy of light into electrical energy that moves a needle across a gauge; the stronger the light the stronger the current and the more the needle moves. These have no batteries to wear out, but in dim light, where exposure is most difficult to estimate, the needle moves little or not at all.

In the other type the current comes from a tiny battery and flows through a cadmium sulfide cell, which acts as a resistor, conducting current and moving a pointer according to the amount of light striking the cell.

Light meters also differ in the way they can be used to measure light. Most hand-held meters—and all built-in ones—are of the reflected-light type, which measures the light reflected from the subject. The meter is pointed at the subject—or at that particular part of the subject the photographer wants to measure at close range—and the reading is made. The light-admitting opening of such meters is restricted—by a hood, a baffle or a faceted lens—so that the angle of view of the meter approximates that of a normal camera lens, about 30° to 50°. In a variation of this type of meter, the angle is reduced to permit more accurate readings of particular parts of the scene. (In some "spot" meters this angle may be as little as a half degree.)

The second type is the incident-light meter, designed to have a much wider angle of view—about 180°—so that it can measure all the light incident on, or falling on, the subject from one side. It gains this wider angle by having a translucent hemisphere of white glass or plastic over the light-measuring cell to diffuse the light. The incident-light meter is held not toward the subject, but toward the light that is falling on the subject from the direction of the camera. Both types of meters generally are provided with two separate scales on the meter face, one to be used in average light and one in very dim light, so that accurate readings can be made under most conditions.

Since each type has advantages under certain circumstances, a number of meters, such as the one shown on the opposite page, are designed so that they can make either reflected or incident readings. When the sensing cell is open to direct light, as illustrated, it serves as a reflected-light meter; when the hemispherical diffuser is slid into position over the sensing cell, it becomes an incident-light meter.

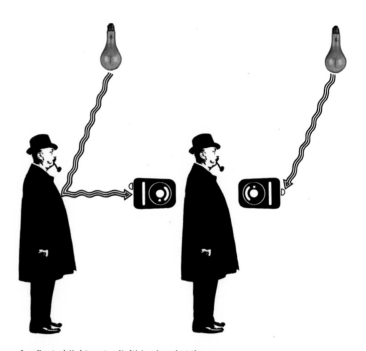

A reflected-light meter (left) is aimed at the subject and measures the light bouncing off the man's clothing. The incident meter (right) is faced away from the subject and toward the camera to measure the general light falling on the man from the direction of the camera.

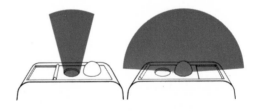

The opening in a reflected-light meter (left) admits light in a limited arc and therefore takes in a small area of the subject when used at close range. The incident meter's coverage, or angle of acceptance (right), is 180°, to enable it to measure all light coming toward the subject from the general direction of the camera.

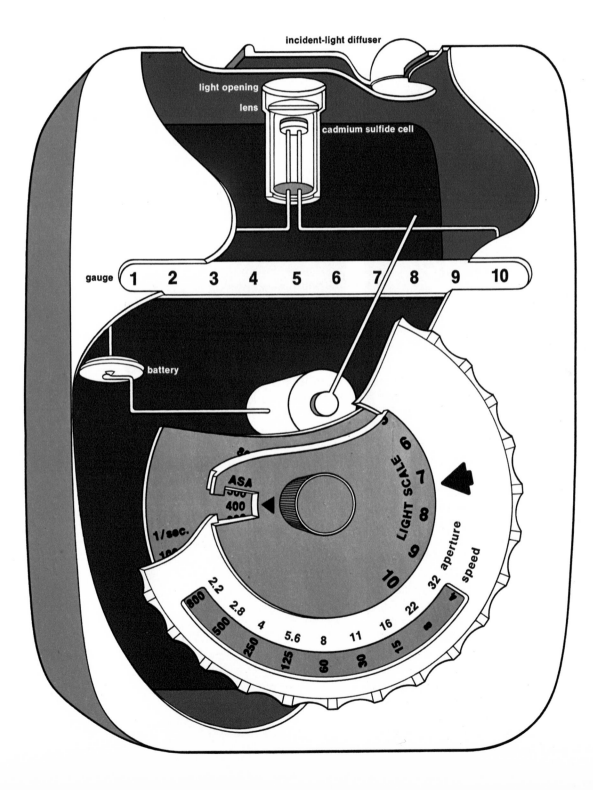

incident-light diffuser

light opening

lens

cadmium sulfide cell

gauge 1 2 3 4 5 6 7 8 9 10

battery

ASA
500
400

1/sec.
100

LIGHT SCALE
6
7
8
9
10

aperture
speed

2.2
2.8
4
5.6
8
11
16
22
32

800
500
250
125
60
30
15

The meter at left is set to measure reflected light. The spherical diffuser, used to make an incident reading, has been slid away from the opening over the sensitive cell. Light enters the opening and passes through a lens to the cadmium sulfide cell. The cell controls the flow of electricity from the battery to a measuring gauge. How much light strikes the cell determines how much current reaches the gauge to move its needle; in this case the reading is slightly over 7. To convert this measurement into an exposure setting, the knob is turned until the ASA rating for the film being used appears in the small window near the center of the dials. Now the large outer dial is turned until its arrow points to the number that had been indicated by the pointer. This pairs aperture with shutter speed (appearing near the bottom edge of the dials) to give correct exposure for the light intensity measured. In this example, correct exposure would be f/2.2 at 1/800 second, f/2.8 at 1/500 second, or any other combination to f/32 at 1/4 second.

The World in Tones of Gray

A light meter doesn't really gauge exposure. It measures light intensity. How that datum eventually determines exposure depends on how the photographer aims to reproduce on film the real world before his camera—a scene that almost always includes many colors of many brightnesses, all of which must be transformed into gray of several shades of brightness. Does he want the sunlit side of a building to appear as a blank white, or as a softer gray with some texture showing? How bright should clouds be? Should only a few tones be captured, or all?

Such questions are not automatically answered by meter readings. They require an interpretive analysis of exposure (often coupled with the use of filters). Such a sophisticated approach to exposure turns out to be simpler than it seems, thanks to the "zone system" developed by the noted California photographer Ansel Adams.

Adams' system is based on a printed "gray scale" like the sample opposite (they can be bought from most camera stores and sometimes come with exposure meters). Its 10 distinct shades of gray show the range of tones, or zones, that the print encompasses. These various zones can be compared—either from memory or from the actual scale —to tones in essential elements of the scene. Then exposure is set to reproduce those elements in desired zones.

The zones are numbered from 0, deep black, resulting from no exposure on the corresponding part of the negative, to 9, paper white, a dense section of the negative. Each succeeding zone (after zone 1) represents a doubling of the exposure of the previous zone—an increase of one f-stop. Obviously, the average tone in the average scene is a medium gray—zone 5—and in the average picture it should appear as zone 5. This is what all reflected-light meters are designed to accomplish; they indicate exposures that will reproduce as zone 5 any light intensity they measure. Only in the middle zones—3 through 7 —is detail clear.

How the zone system helps determine exposure can be seen in the picture opposite, on which numbers indicate the zones for various areas. The light shadows under the decks are zone 5 and a reflected-light meter reading of this area would have indicated the exposure for this negative. This exposure gave detail in the cloth cover (zone 2), but made the stairs (zone 9) too bright for clarity and the reflection of the hull (zone 1) too dark. Suppose some detail had been essential in the zone 1 reflection. By opening the lens one stop, the photographer would have shifted one zone up the scale, making some slight detail visible. But all other areas would be lightened similarly; zone 0 might disappear, and the zone 8 wall area would probably be indistinguishable from the stairs which are in zone 9.

This picture suffers no lack of detail. Its magnificent range of tonal values, 0 through 9, provides not only the accents of the extreme tones but also rich shades in the middle zones where the most detail can be readily accommodated. This full-scale rendition is generally the aim of the photographer, simply because it does make available more usable tones. But in some scenes only a few tones are of interest, and only they need be reproduced. The zone system can be used to interpret light-meter readings for either result.

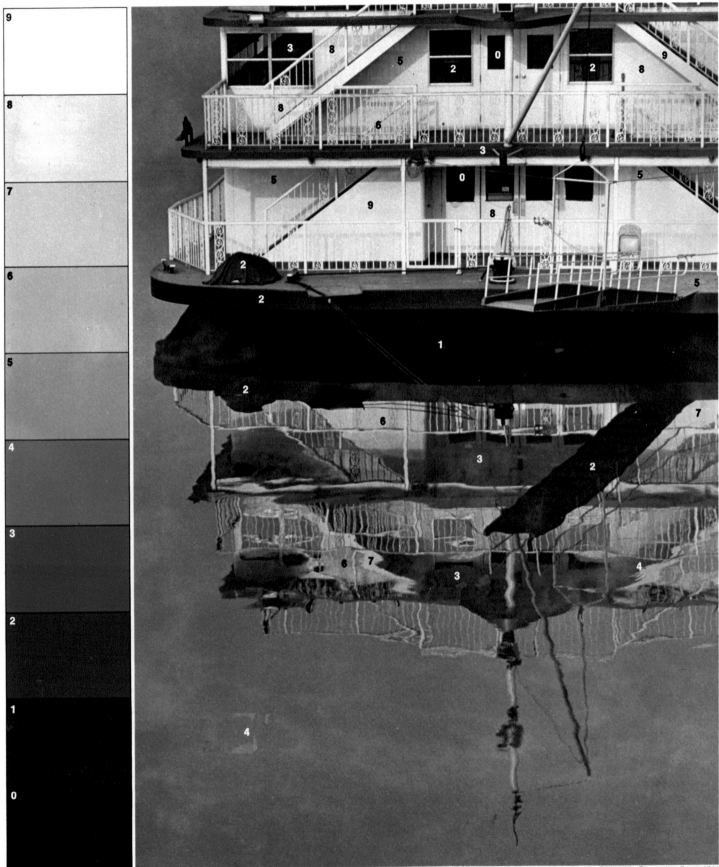

DAVID VAN DEVEER: *Excursion Boat*, 1968

Eliminating Tones with Filters

Reflections from glass or water *(below, left)* are tones a photographer may wish to avoid in his picture. They can be eliminated very simply because they are made up of light that is unusual in that it is polarized; i.e., the waves are oriented at one angle rather than many angles *(pages 20-21)*. This makes it possible to control them with a polarizing filter, which can block light oriented at one angle and thus also block the reflections *(below, right)*.

A polarizing filter looks transparent but contains submicroscopic crystals lined up like parallel slats. Light waves that are parallel to the crystals pass between them; waves oriented at other angles are obstructed by the crystals,

as indicated in the diagram at right. Since the polarized light is all at the same angle, the filter can be turned to block it. This also blocks some waves in the general scene light, but only those oriented like polarized light; the rest get through.

To find the orientation that will block polarized light, the photographer looks through the filter and rotates it until the unwanted reflection vanishes. The filter is then placed in the same position over the lens. (With a single-lens reflex camera, the filter can be adjusted while it is in place over the lens.) Because of the partial blockage of light by the filter, the aperture must be opened 1⅓ stops above the normal exposure. □

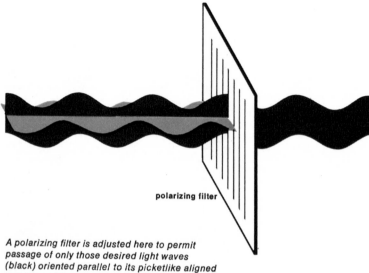

polarizing filter

A polarizing filter is adjusted here to permit passage of only those desired light waves (black) oriented parallel to its picketlike aligned crystals and to screen out all other light waves (gray) angled across the pickets.

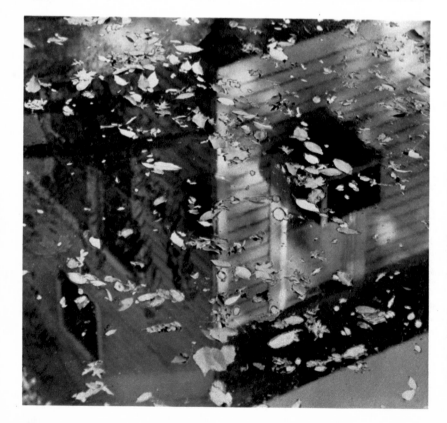

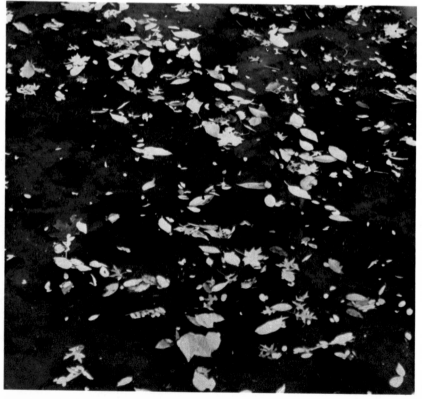

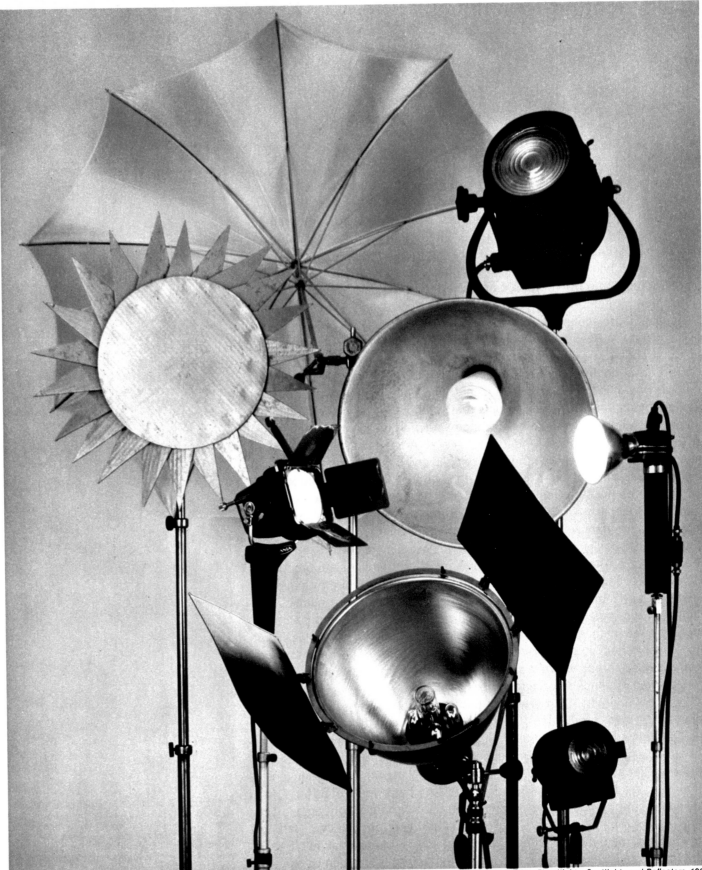

HOWARD HARRISON: *Floodlights, Spotlights and Reflectors,* 1968

181

An Interplay of Lighted Images

Christopher Wren, the architect whose buildings transformed London after the Great Fire of 1666, had a genius for harmonies of design. When LIFE photographer Mark Kauffman set out to do a study of Wren's famous churches, he conveyed their harmony by combining several examples—widely separated in space—into a single photograph.

First Kauffman took Polaroid pictures of the individual churches and used them to compose his photograph in advance, cutting out the spires from each picture and arranging and rearranging them on a large piece of paper. When he had settled on the best composition, he photographed the building that was to be the centerpiece, the massive dome of St. Paul's, using a 4 x 5 Graphic view camera. By shooting at dusk, he easily isolated its bulk from its surroundings. Then he proceeded to photograph the other churches on the same sheet of Ektachrome B film. But to single out these smaller towers from their surroundings and make them stand out and against the dark central dome and sky in the final picture, Kauff-man had to light them individually at night, and this posed some problems he had not counted on.

In order to illuminate the church spires strongly enough, several 10,000-watt spotlights and a portable generator were needed. The London police gave him permission to set up these lights in the streets, but traffic and curious crowds made his work difficult nonetheless. To get a clear view of the towers over surrounding trees and rooftops, Kauffman took his pictures from a "cherry picker," a mobile scaffold of the kind used by utility repairmen. Each night Kauffman set up his scaffold and lights at a picture-taking site, but at least twice the preparations were in vain—a dense London fog rolled in and made work impossible. When conditions were right and the exposure was made, Kauffman moved on to the next site, sometimes to endure additional frustration. In the end, his labor paid off: the photograph of seven church spires, dominated by St. Paul's, suggests the "compleat Beauty" that Wren made his own goal.

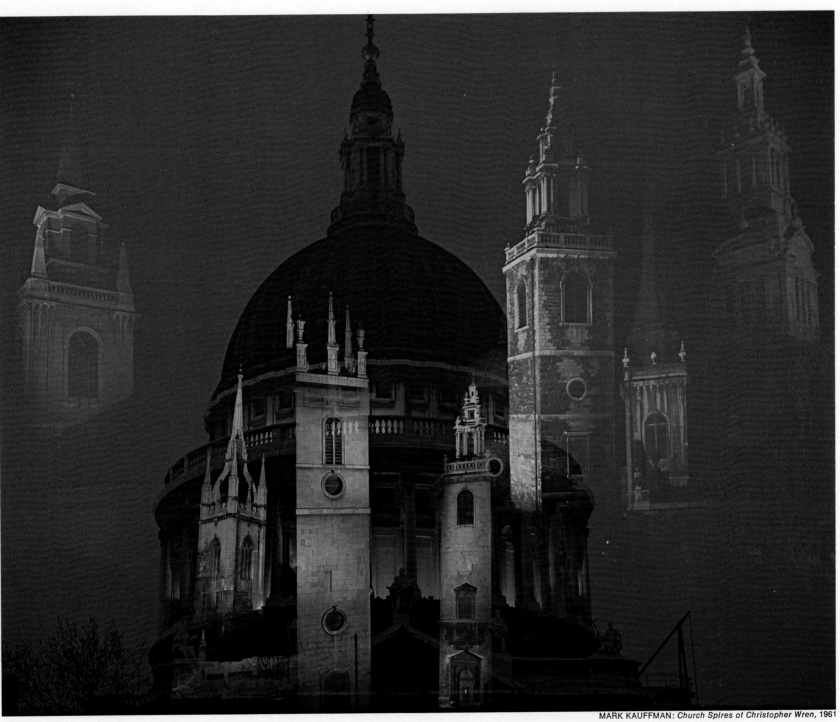

MARK KAUFFMAN: *Church Spires of Christopher Wren*, 1961

Relighting a Fire with Flash

The catastrophic fire that swept through the fashionable Bel Air section of Los Angeles in 1961 left some $50 million worth of damage in its wake, a number of Hollywood stars homeless and a landscape reminiscent of a bombed city. The desolate scene was given an extra dimension by LIFE's Ralph Crane with an adroit use of flash bulbs, which he deployed to suggest an after-dark holocaust while revealing the devastation the fire left behind.

On a ridge overlooking a burned-out hillside, Crane set up two cameras: one a 4 x 5 Speed Graphic loaded with Polaroid Land film to make test exposures, the other a 4 x 5 Linhof view camera, with which he made the picture at right—10 separate exposures on a single piece of Ektachrome B film. Crane's two assistants, each carrying a hand-operated flash gun and a pocketful of powerful No. 22 bulbs, spread out along the rows of charred houses. They were alerted to move and to fire their flashes on signals from Crane, who blew a whistle every time he wanted them to move forward. When they had reached a spot that the photographer wished to highlight in his photograph, he opened his lens, then blew his whistle again as a signal that the flash bulbs should be set off. (The assistants kept out of range of the camera by taking cover in the rubble.) Crane made simultaneous exposures with both cameras; when he had finished he found two unlighted areas on the Polaroid print, so he sent his assistants back to those spots and made two more exposures.

Crane might have used portable electronic flashlights for his picture, setting off 20 or so simultaneously in different locations, but he decided that they would produce a relatively weak flash with too narrow a beam for the effect he wanted. By using powerful flash bulbs mounted in flat reflectors, he was able to spread a great deal of light across an arc of 180°. And with the flashes covered by red filters, each wide-sweeping burst of light created the grim illusion of an inferno still raging in the center of each house. By making 10 exposures of two seconds each, Crane provided enough light to be able to stop his lens down to f/11 for depth of field and still record the twinkling lights of Los Angeles that can be seen here in the background.

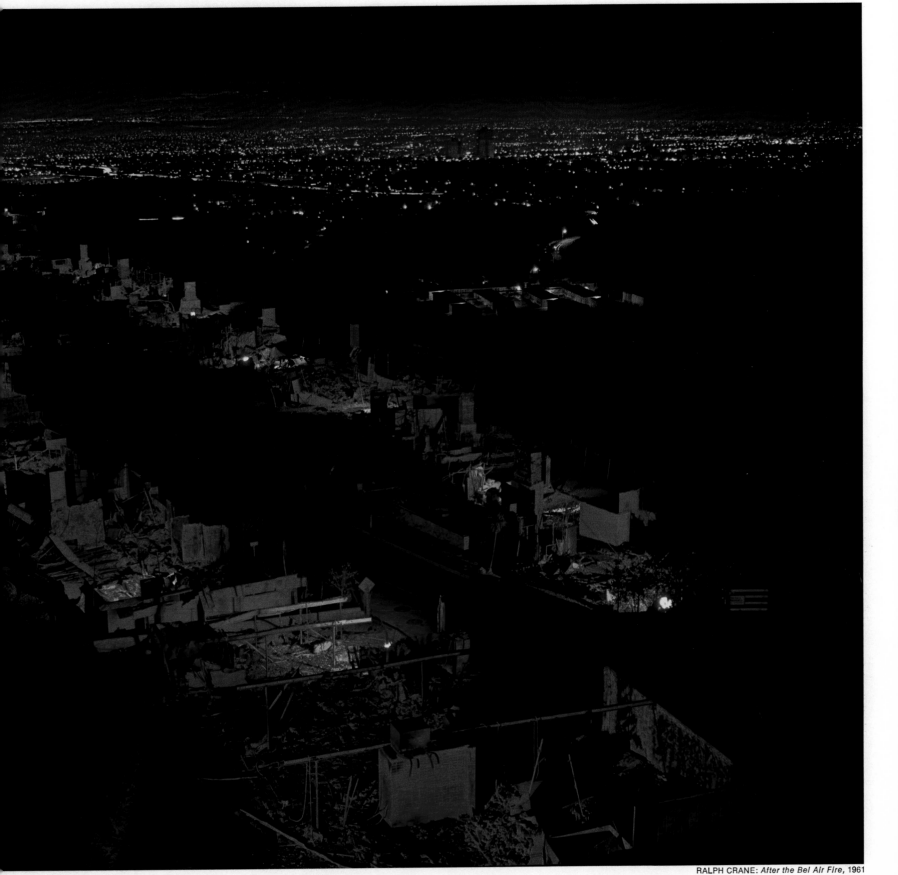

RALPH CRANE: *After the Bel Air Fire*, 1961

Using Light to Create Movement

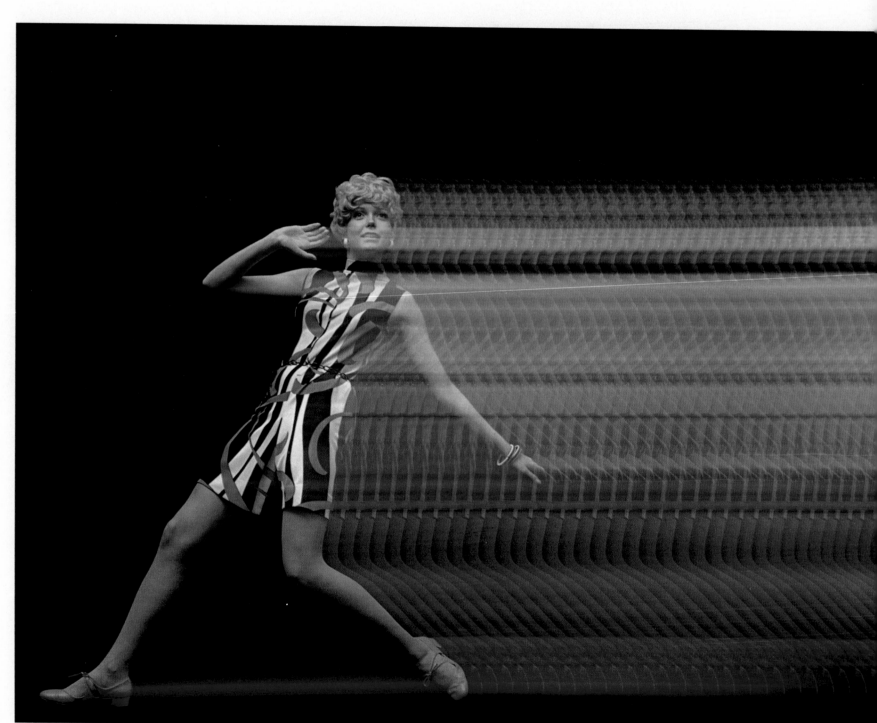

BEN ROSE: *Model in "Motion,"* 1968

Repetitive flashes of light are often used by photographers to divide a motion into a series of steps that reveal the sequence of the action—the intricacies of a ballet dancer's rapid movements, the course of a curve ball as it speeds from the pitcher's mound to the plate. Photographer Ben Rose, on the other hand, sometimes employs the rapidly pulsing electronic flash in exactly the opposite way: to build up an illusion of motion where none actually exists.

The fashion models in the pictures shown here were photographed standing absolutely still against a black velvet background; their apparent motion is created in the camera. For the picture at left, Rose used four stroboscopic lights and adjusted them to fire at a rate of six times a second. His camera was attached to a special mount and an electric motor moved it sideways at an even rate. As the camera panned, Rose opened the shutter for about two seconds, a period during which the successive flashes exposed a series of some 48 images. For the picture at right, in which the girl seems to be moving toward the camera, he used a zoom lens and both zoomed and panned while the lights flashed on and off. The change in size of the figure in successive images is the result of the changing focal length of the lens.

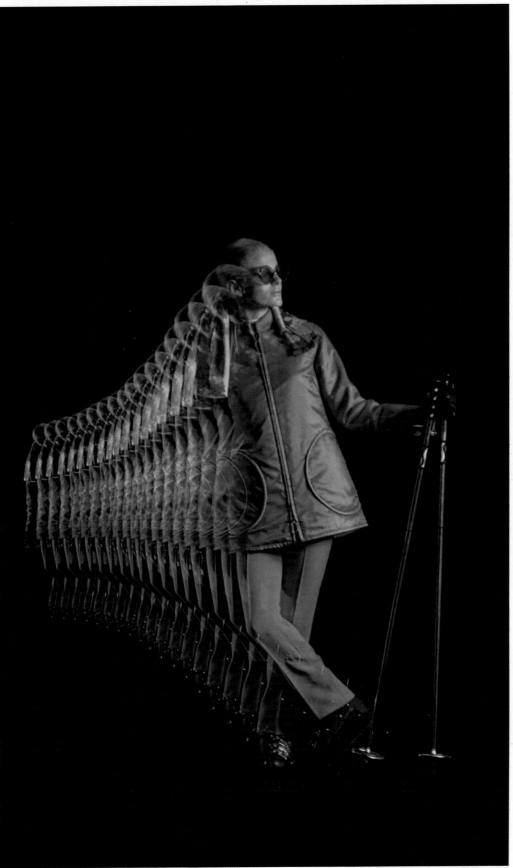

BEN ROSE: *Style for Skiing,* 1969

209

Lighting for a Knockout

Suddenly the fight was over. Halfway through the first round in Lewiston, Maine, heavyweight challenger Sonny Liston lay motionless on the canvas. Towering above him in the referee's restraining embrace was the young, scornful champion Muhammad Ali (Cassius Clay), taunting his opponent to get up and fight. The knockout happened so fast that most of the crowd, including many of the ringside photographers, never even saw the shattering punch that put Liston down. But Neil Leifer of SPORTS ILLUSTRATED, anticipating a knockout—though not necessarily of the favored Liston—had been preparing for such a moment for several days.

Leifer's motorized Nikon F camera, which automatically advances the film after each exposure, was mounted on the framework holding the floodlights directly above the ring (the announc-er's microphone can be seen at center dangling from the same framework). The camera was equipped with an 8mm fisheye lens to take in a field of 180 degrees. Leifer's biggest problem was to provide enough light to cover the whole crowd and to permit the fast shutter speed needed to freeze the swift central action. He had assembled a set of 40 electronic flash units to supplement the arena's illumination system. Several flash units were mounted on the framework along with the camera; others were hung from the arena's ceiling.

Leifer chose his moment carefully, since he had to wait 25 to 30 seconds between exposures for the lights to recharge. He chose well. While shooting closeups with another camera at ringside 150 feet below, he had an assistant trip the shutter by remote control to catch one of the most dramatic moments in modern ring history.

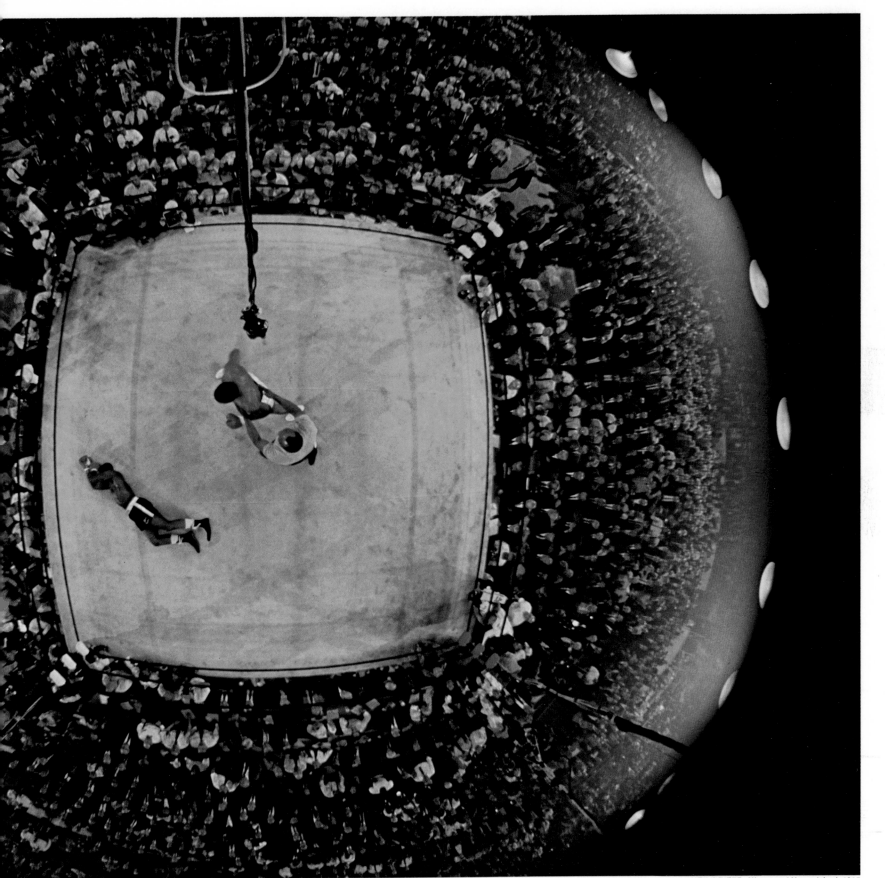

NEIL LEIFER: *Victor and Vanquished*, 1965

Total Lighting

Among the biggest lighting jobs to challenge the resourcefulness of LIFE photographers was the task of covering the historic visit of Pope Paul VI to America in 1965. Two of the high points of the Pope's visit were scheduled within hours of each other, one indoors, the other at an outdoor arena at night.

The vast, dim interior of St. Patrick's Cathedral in New York was the scene of the first religious ceremony ever conducted in America by a reigning pope. To get a color picture of the Pontiff's entrance Yale Joel needed every bit of light he could get. By placing 50 large portable electronic flash units around the upper gallery, he was able to create enough illumination to record the historic moment *(right)*. However, his use of almost all of LIFE's equipment meant that the next great event, a mass at Yankee Stadium, would have to be lighted some other way.

Ralph Morse, who drew the Stadium assignment, could count on one major assist. There was already plenty of light at the center of the scene, because the television networks had focused an array of powerful beams on the altar so that they could cover the ceremony. But Morse wanted to include a sizeable portion of the 90,000 onlookers in the picture as well, and he had to supplement the television lights with floodlights aimed at the crowd. To match the intense light at the center of the stadium, he was forced to use more than 100 lights of his own, mounted above the crowds in the dark areas of the balconies. His painstaking preparations were rewarded by a photograph *(opposite)* that dramatically conveyed the spectacle of thousands of worshippers being led by the Pope in prayer.

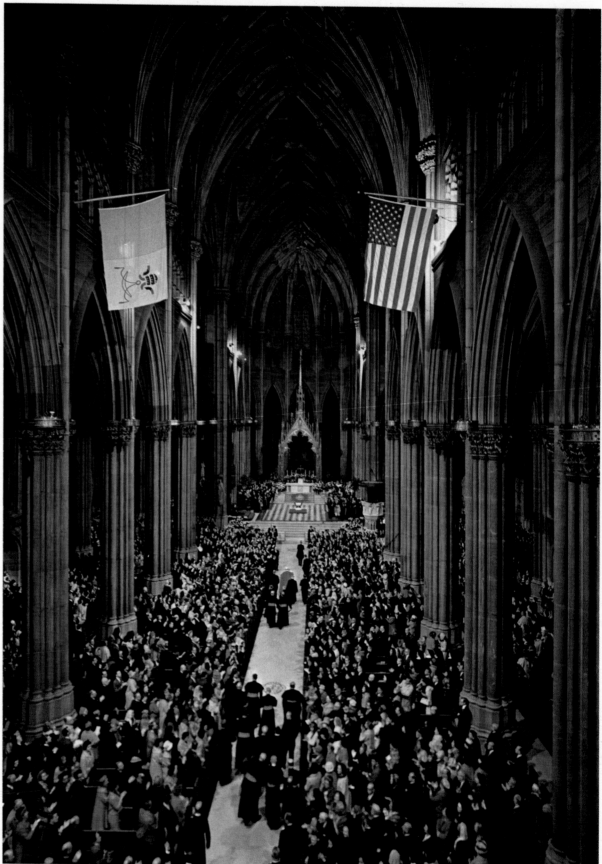

YALE JOEL: *Pope Paul VI Entering St. Patrick's Cathedral,* 1965

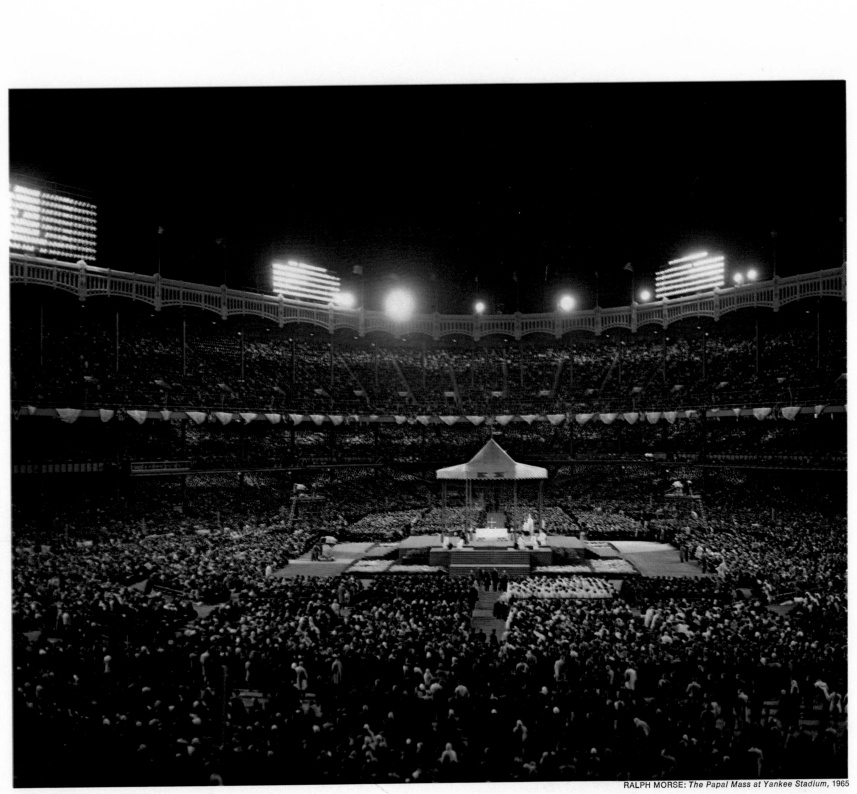

RALPH MORSE: *The Papal Mass at Yankee Stadium,* 1965

213

Blending Natural and Artificial Light

In the pictures shown here, photographer Arnold Newman balanced natural light and artificial light to achieve two quite different effects. For a portrait of the German industrialist and former arms manufacturer Alfried Krupp von Bohlen und Halbach, Newman sought to suggest the evil symbolized by this wartime master of slave labor. He posed Krupp in the grim surroundings of one of his factories. Daylight filtered in through grimy skylights and two spotlights (fitted with blue filters to match their color with that of the daylight) were placed low to cast harsh shadows on Krupp's face. To heighten the effect of the lighting, Newman took advantage of a characteristic of daylight color film—the tendency of its color rendition to be altered by long exposure time. The dim illumination called for an exposure of more than a second. That was enough to produce a greenish cast in the skin, adding to the aura of malevolence.

Newman's more flattering portrait of architect Louis Kahn *(opposite)* posed another delicate exercise in balancing light. Newman wanted to show Kahn against both the interior and exterior of his glass-walled art gallery at Yale University and decided to shoot the picture at dusk when the inside lights were on but the fading rays of the sun still lighted the façade. He chose indoor-type color film, which is color-balanced to suit both the colors emitted by the building's incandescent lights and the two spotlights used to illuminate the architect's face. It is not color-balanced for daylight, however. The result was a face warm and natural against the cool, blue-tinged background lighted by the rays of the fading sun.

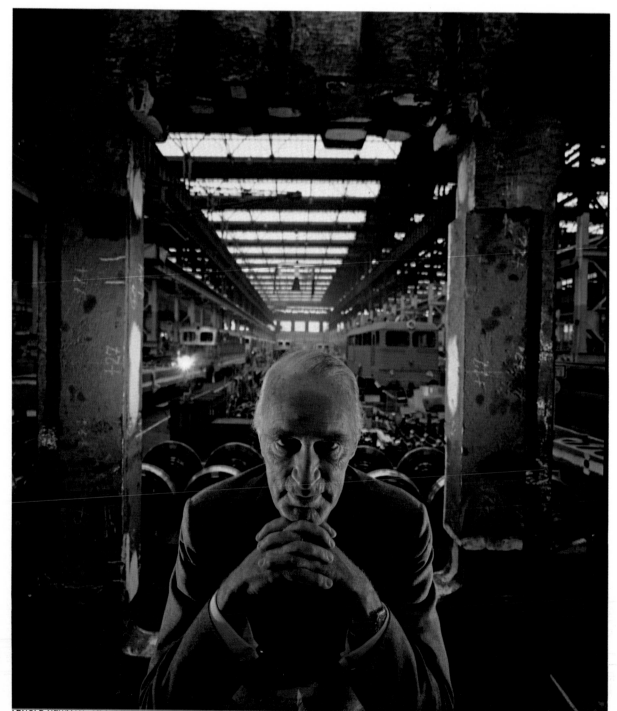

ARNOLD NEWMAN: *Alfried Krupp von Bohlen und Halbach,* 1963

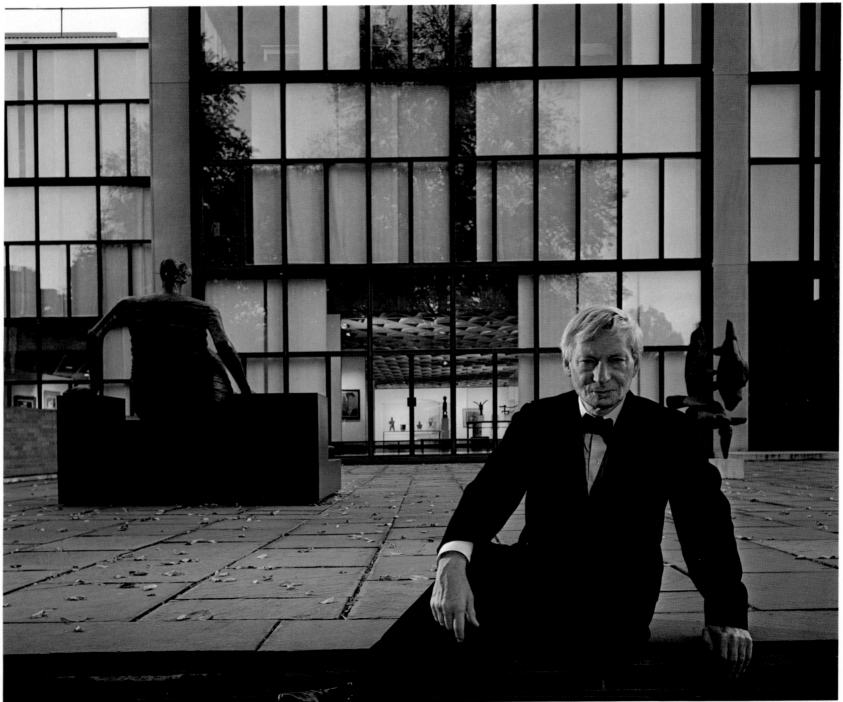

ARNOLD NEWMAN: *Louis Kahn*, 1964

Balancing Light in Two Worlds

LIFE's George Silk needed both ingenuity and luck to get this view of two forms of wildlife sharing a stream in Montana. He set up near the stream to photograph rainbow trout with a camera mounted in a partially submerged box with a glass front *(diagram below)*. But soon after he began work he noticed that a fawn came to drink from the stream every day late in the afternoon. He immediately saw the potential for an extraordinary photograph that would show fish and deer together. The light in the underwater realm of the trout, however, was far dimmer than that in the sun-splashed world above. In order to achieve a balance, Silk set a single electronic flash unit beside the stream and aimed it down on the water. He placed it close enough to the surface to make the illumination cast underwater match the quality of the daylight at the hour of the deer's visit. Finally, after weeks of on-and-off waiting, the lighting conditions and the animal participants came together. With high-speed Ektachrome in a Hasselblad camera, the shutter set at 1/60 second and the lens at f/22 (for maximum depth of field), Silk was ready. He recalls, "The fawn was a perfect actor—he walked over to the stream, drank and looked around, and I had time to take several shots before he disappeared."

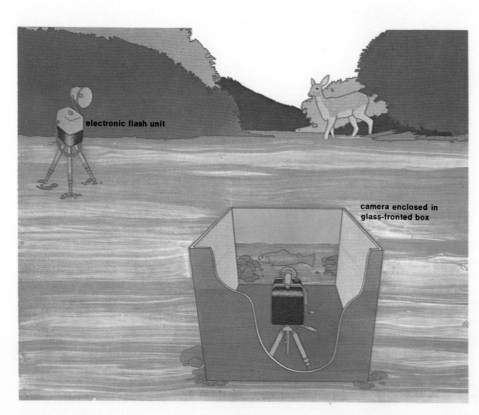

electronic flash unit

camera enclosed in glass-fronted box

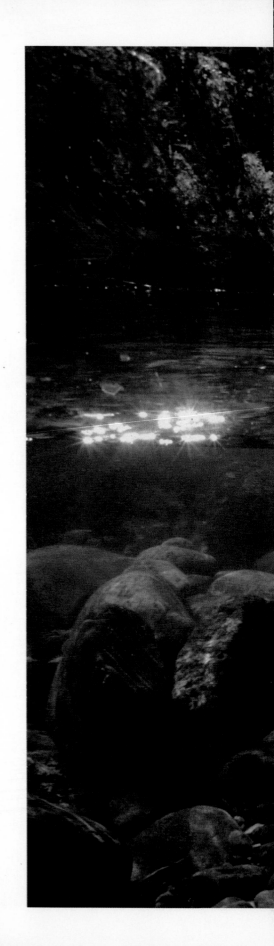

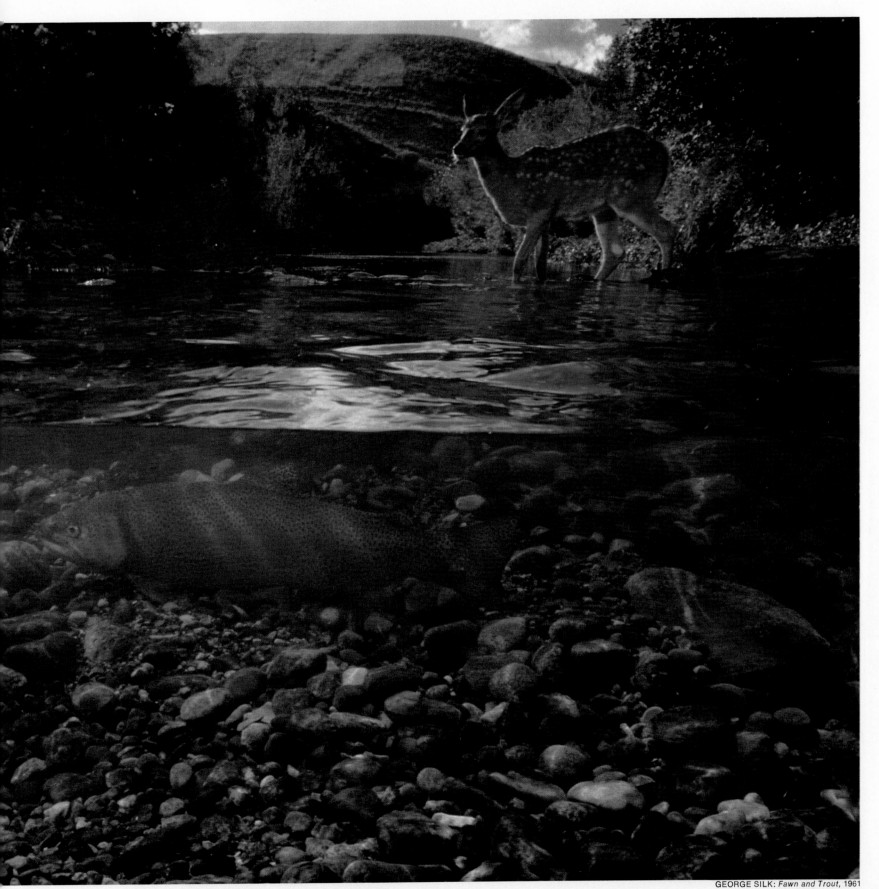

GEORGE SILK: *Fawn and Trout,* 1961

Capturing a Laser's Own Light

In the early 1960s the editors of LIFE assigned Fritz Goro to do a story on the laser beam, then just beginning to attract public attention for its potential in fields as diverse as communications and surgery. Laser light, unlike ordinary light, disperses relatively little, even over long distances, and thus can be directed with pinpoint accuracy. This precisely focused energy is now often used in operations on human eyes, to weld detached retinas into place, a technique perfected through experiments with animals.

When Goro decided to photograph a rabbit undergoing such an experimental operation, the scientists involved declared the task virtually impossible because of the difficulty in capturing the laser beam itself on film. Their laser consisted of a rod, made of synthetic

ruby, that emitted a thin beam of red light when struck by the white light of an electronic flash tube. The beam lasted only a few thousandths of a second and Goro found that it could not be seen under normal laboratory light conditions. However, he knew the laser beam could be made visible by passing it through a field of smoke—if the smoke was of exactly the right density.

Goro had a special box built *(diagram below),* to contain the rabbit and the smoke. He then generated smoke by burning briquettes of incense and fed this into the chamber with a tiny blower. After dozens of test exposures, Goro found the right combination of film (fast indoor Ektachrome), aperture f/8, and smoke density. The result, seen at right, was one of the first photographs ever taken of a laser in action.

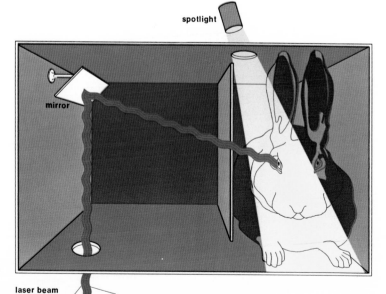

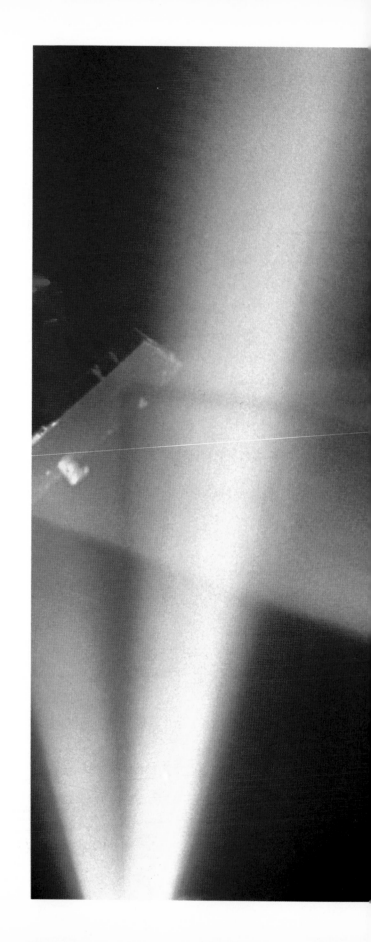

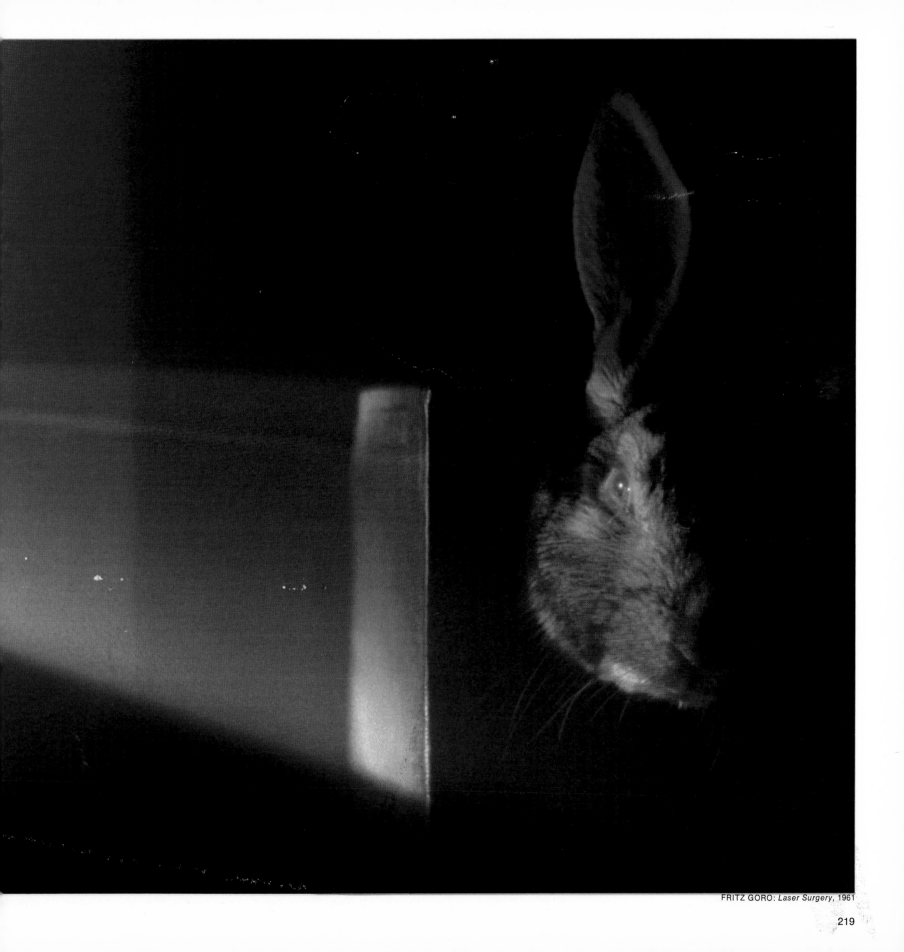

Piping Light Inside the Body

Lennart Nilsson, a Swedish photographer renowned for pictures made inside the human body, has taken the camera's eye into such hidden realms as the womb and the twisting tunnel of an artery. One of his most exacting photographic forays was made into the middle ear—a region barely as large as a sugar cube.

The picture at right shows the ear from the inside looking out toward the eardrum. Taken during an autopsy, it reveals the exquisite engineering of the three small bones—called the hammer, anvil and stirrup—that transmit vibrations from the eardrum to a sensing organ. The picture was made with a tiny fisheye lens mounted on the end of a thin hollow tube; this lens projected the image to a second, larger lens, a half inch in diameter, that magnified the image 20 times and sent it onto the film.

To pipe light into the small cavity, Nilsson used flexible cords made up of many thin glass fibers. Light, picked up at one end of the cord, travels along the fibers much like water moving through a hose, and comes out the other end.

Nilsson used two cords, each carrying light from a 150-watt bulb of the type used in slide projectors; one was placed just behind the fisheye lens and the other on the outer side of the eardrum. To compensate for the slightly greenish light cast by the cords, he used a pink filter on his lens. Though not usually given to complimenting his own work, even Nilsson was impressed by the result, pronouncing the picture of the middle ear "unbelievable." □

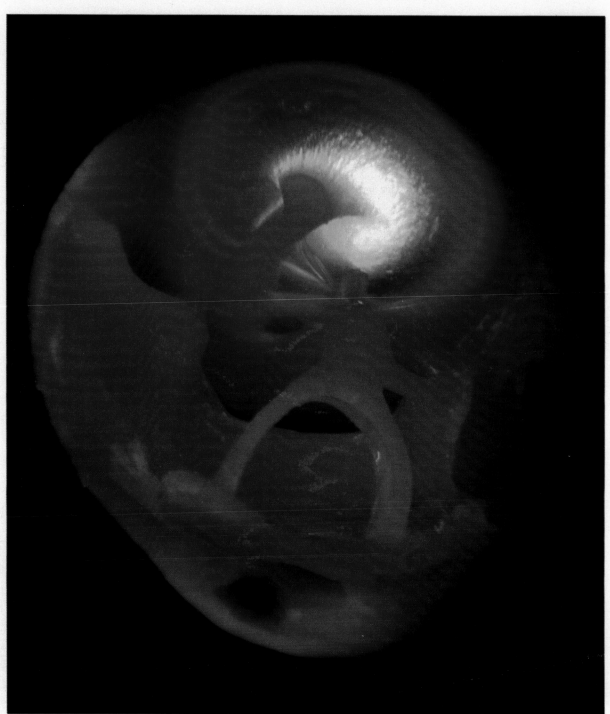

LENNART NILSSON: *The Middle Ear*, 1969

Bibliography

General

Feininger, Andreas, *The Creative Photographer.* Prentice-Hall, 1955.

Focal Press Ltd., *Focal Encyclopedia of Photography.* McGraw-Hill, 1959.

Neblette, Carroll B., *Photography: Its Materials and Processes.* Van Nostrand, 1962.

Rhode, Robert B., and Floyd H. McCall, *Introduction to Photography.* Macmillan, 1965.

Sussman, Aaron, *The Amateur Photographer's Handbook.* Thomas Y. Crowell, 1965.

History

Darrah, William Culp, *Stereo Views: A History of Stereographs in America and Their Collection.* Times and News Publishing, 1964.

*Eder, Josef Maria, *History of Photography.* Columbia University Press, 1945.

Gardner, Alexander, *Gardner's Photographic Sketch Book of the Civil War.* Dover Publications, 1959.

Gernsheim, Helmut, *History of Photography.* Oxford University Press, 1955.

Gernsheim, Helmut, and Alison, *L.J.M. Daguerre: The History of the Diorama and the Daguerreotype.* Secker and Warburg, 1956.

Newhall, Beaumont:
The Daguerreotype in America. Duell, Sloan and Pearce, 1961.
The History of Photography from 1839 to the Present Day. The Museum of Modern Art, Doubleday, 1964.

Pollack, Peter, *The Picture History of Photography.* Harry N. Abrams, 1958.

†Taft, Robert, *Photography and the American Scene.* Dover Publications, 1964.

Biography

Barnett, Lincoln, *The Universe and Dr. Einstein.* William Sloane Associates, 1948.

Gernsheim, Helmut, and Alison, *Roger Fenton, Photographer of the Crimean War.* Secker and Warburg, 1954.

Horan, James D.:
Mathew Brady, Historian with a Camera. Crown Publishers, 1955.
Timothy O'Sullivan, America's Forgotten Photographer. Doubleday, 1966.

Jackson, Clarence S., *Picture Maker of the Old West, William H. Jackson.* Scribner, 1947.

Special Fields

Adams, Ansel:
Polaroid Land Photography Manual. Morgan & Morgan, 1963.
The Negative. Morgan & Morgan, 1968.

Eastman Kodak:
†*Applied Infrared Photography.* Eastman Kodak, 1968.
Filters for Black and White and Color Pictures. Eastman Kodak, 1969.
Flash Pictures. Eastman Kodak, 1967.
†*Kodak Black-and-White Films in Rolls.* Eastman Kodak, 1967.

Eaton, George T., *Photographic Chemistry.* Morgan & Morgan, 1965.

Hackforth, Henry L., *Infrared Radiation.* McGraw-Hill, 1960.

Jacobs, Lou Jr., *Electronic Flash.* American Photographic Book Publishing Co., 1962.

Massy, H.S.W., and R.L.F. Boyd, *The Upper Atmosphere.* Philosophical Library, 1958.

Mees, C.E. Kenneth, *From Dry Plates to Ektachrome Film.* Ziff-Davis, 1961.

Mees, C.E. Kenneth, and T.H. James, *The Theory of the Photographic Process.* Macmillan, 1966.

Mueller, Conrad G., and Mae Rudolph and the Editors of TIME-LIFE Books, *Light and Vision.* TIME-LIFE Books, 1969.

Newhall, Beaumont, *Airborne Camera, The World from the Air and Outer Space.* Hastings House, 1969.

Smith, Alpheus W., and John N. Cooper, *Elements of Physics.* McGraw-Hill, 1964.

White, Minor, *The Zone System Manual.* Morgan & Morgan, 1968.

Magazines

Aperture, Aperture Inc., New York City
British Journal of Photography, Henry Greenwood and Co., London
Camera, C.J. Bucher Ltd., Lucerne, Switzerland
Camera 35, U.S. Camera Publishing Co., New York City
Creative Camera, International Federation of Amateur Photographers, London
Infinity, American Society of Magazine Photographers, New York City
Modern Photography, The Billboard Publishing Co., New York City
Popular Photography, Ziff-Davis Publishing Co., New York City
Travel & Camera, U.S. Camera Publishing Corp., New York City
U.S. Camera World Annual, U.S. Camera Publishing Corp., New York City

*Also available in paperback.
†Available only in paperback.

Acknowledgments

For help given in the preparation of this book, the editors are indebted to Myles Adler, Public Relations Department, AGFA-Gevaert, Inc., Teterboro, New Jersey; Photography Archives, Art Institute of Chicago, Chicago, Illinois; Norbert S. Baer, Institute of Fine Arts, New York University, New York City; Samuel Berkey, President, Berkey Photo, Inc., New York City; Richard O. Berube, Publicity Department, Polaroid Corporation, Cambridge, Massachusetts; Robert E. Bilbey, Manager, Advertising and Sales Promotion Department and Richard Craig, Aerospace Product Specialist, Weston Instruments, Inc., Newark, New Jersey; Priscilla Bresbery, Society of Illuminating Engineers, New York City; Josephine Cobb, Specialist in Iconography, General Services Administration, National Archives and Records Service, Washington, D.C.; Glen F. Cruze, Application Engineer, Mallory Battery Co., Tarrytown, New York; Peter Denzer, Brooklyn, New York; Stanley Erinwein, Tiffen Manufacturing Corp., Roslyn Heights, New York; George Eastman House, Rochester, New York; Fritz Goro, Chappaqua, New York; David Haberstich, Museum Specialist, Section of Photography, The Smithsonian Institution, Washington, D.C.; James Hartnett, Supervisor, Photographic Service Department, Polaroid Corp., Cambridge, Massachusetts; James D. Horan, Weehawken, New Jersey; Mel Ingber, Bellerose, New York; Charles C. Irby, Assistant Curator, Photographic Collections, The Gernsheim Collection, Humanities Research Center, University of Texas, Austin; Kling Photo Corp., Woodside, New York; David S. Lewandowski, Product Publicity Section, GAF Corp., New York; John W. Mathewson, Manager, General Sales, Herbick & Held Printing Co., Pittsburgh, Pennsylvania; Edward Murphy, Consumer Relations Department, Ehrenreich Photo-Optical Industries, Inc., Garden City, New York; Allan Porter, Editor, *Camera* magazine, Lucerne, Switzerland; William P. Ryan, Vice President, Calumet Manufacturing Co., Chicago, Illinois; Patricia Savoia and Elfriede Merman, The Manhattan Ballet School, New York City; Leonard Soned, New York City; William F. Swann, Manager, Professional, Commercial and Industrial Division, Eastman Kodak Co., Rochester, New York; John L. Tupper, Cousin's Island, Yarmouth, Maine; Robert Walch, Brooklyn, New York; Joel Snyder, Chicago, Illinois; David Vestal, Assoc. Editor, *Travel and Camera* and *Camera 35,* U.S. Camera Publishing Co., New York City; Peter Wehmann, Account Executive, Needham, Harper & Steers, Inc., New York City; Paul Wentz, Photographic Division, Honeywell, Inc., Long Island City, New York.

Index *Numerals in italics indicate a photograph, painting or drawing of the subject mentioned.*

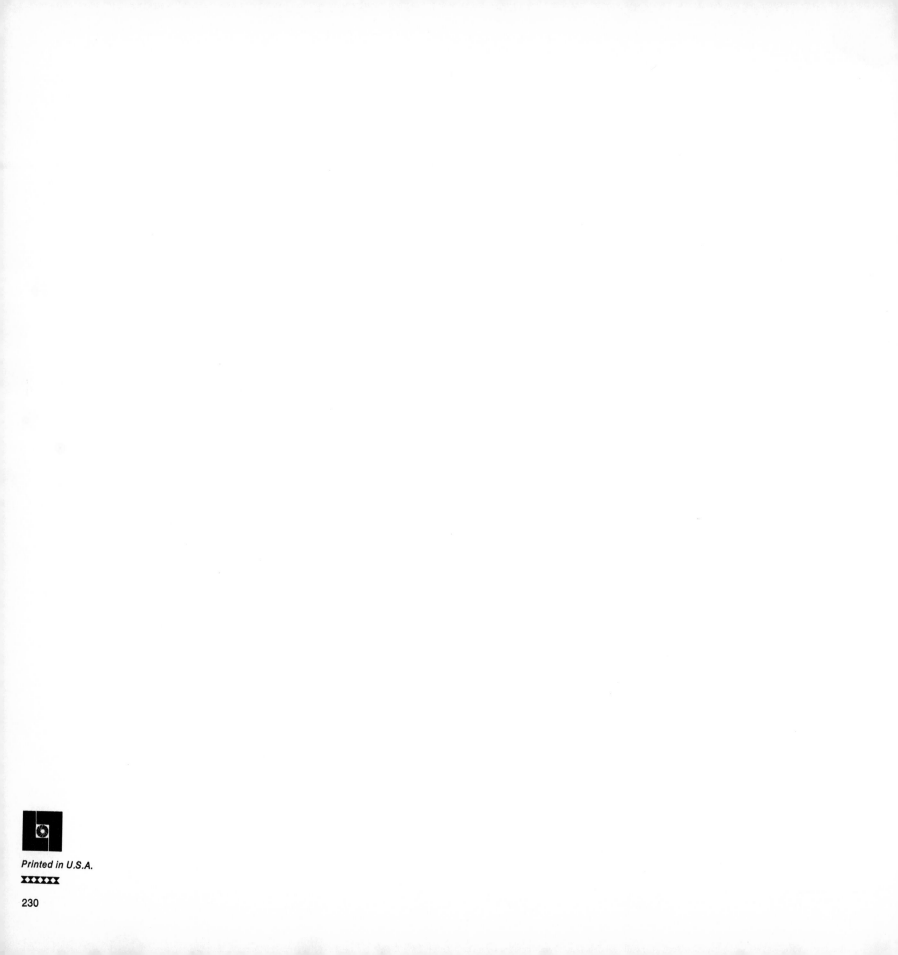

Printed in U.S.A.